The Nature of Design

A

QUILT

ARTIST'S

PERSONAL

JOURNAL

—

Joan Colvin

**FIBER
STUDIO
PRESS**

An Imprint of
That Patchwork Place

FIBER STUDIO PRESS

The Nature of Design
©1996 by Joan Colvin

That Patchwork Place, Inc.
PO Box 118
Bothell, WA 98041-0118 USA

Printed in Hong Kong
01 00 99 98 97 96   6 5 4 3 2 1

Credits

Editorial Director ...... Kerry I. Hoffman

Technical Editor .... Melissa Lowe

Managing Editor .... Greg Sharp

Copy Editor .... Liz McGehee

Proofreader .... Melissa Riesland

Illustrator .... Brian Metz

Photographer .... Brent Kane
(unless otherwise noted)

Design Director .... Judy Petry

Text & Cover Designer .... Kay Green

Production Assistant .... Shean Bemis

Library of Congress
Cataloging-in-Publication Data

Colvin, Joan,
      The nature of design / Joan Colvin.
          p.   cm.
      ISBN 1-56477-131-8
      1. Quilts—Design. 2. Quilting.
      3. Nature (Aesthetics) I. Title.
      TT835.C6477   1996
      746.46—dc20   96-3199
                                   CIP

MISSION STATEMENT

WE ARE DEDICATED TO PROVIDING
QUALITY PRODUCTS AND SERVICES
THAT INSPIRE CREATIVITY.

WE WORK TOGETHER TO ENRICH
THE LIVES WE TOUCH.

*That Patchwork Place is a financially
responsible ESOP company.*

Contents

Acknowledgments

Thanks to my small group, Quilters on the Edge. Hazel Ayre Hynds has generously shared her considerable knowledge of quiltmaking, past and present, and has given me direction and support. Nell Clinton Moynihan's art studies led to refreshing discussions. Suzanne Hammond has helped with teaching expertise and quiltmaking techniques. And I am always grateful to Betty Oves and Kim Radder for their honest, helpful critiques.

Thanks to the organizations whose newsletters I receive, especially the Association of Pacific Northwest Quilters, the Contemporary QuiltArt Association, the Studio Art Quilt Association, and the Canada Quilt Study Group. The members of these organizations put their own work aside and shared vital information with all of us interested in the art-quilt movement.

Thanks to local shop owners Mary Hales, Julie Petrzelk and Emily Nelson, Sharon and Jason Yenter, and others who let me try teaching in supportive atmospheres.

Thanks to my students, especially my most loyal one, Pat Goffette. Pat patiently worked and waited for the creative muses to inspire her. They have. Her thoughtful help, both inside and outside of class, is greatly appreciated.

Thanks to Judi Warren, who improved my understanding of transparency (although she may wonder if anything "took"). Ann Johnston's dye-painting class was wonderful. Lois Ericson inspires me. I'm looking forward to a class with Ruth McDowell.

Thanks to the following people who provided wonderful hand-dyed fabrics: Alaska Dyeworks; FLAIR, Marlis Kuusela; Carol Olson; Judy Robertson; and the talented dyers whose work I bought before I began to take notes on sources.

Very special thanks to Melissa Lowe and all the people at That Patchwork Place, who are very good at what they do. They are part of the glue that bonds fabric lovers together throughout the world.

Thanks to some helpful neighbors, especially Mary Lee Mains and Janene Kenaston.

Thanks to my sister, Judy Slattery, her husband, Frank, and my mother, Dorothy Chase McClane, who continue to be my emotional support and my most provocative critics.

Thanks to our children: Scott, Annie, and Ellen. Our experiences together flavor my work and continue to teach me the wonders of family life.

And, most of all, thanks and love to my husband, Bill, who cares enough to fuss over my wavering attention to duty, yet makes everything possible, as always.

Introduction

When I discovered quiltmaking in 1988, my experience in other areas of art and my lifetime love of fabric seemed to coalesce. In retrospect, I think a pivotal point in my work occurred in 1989, when I purchased a book on the work of Japanese artist Ayako Miyawaki. I was stunned by her simple but heartstoppingly powerful treatment of nature. Although the book was written in Japanese, I never felt that a translation was needed. For me, her work was language.

While writing this book, I found a statement from Ayako's exhibition in this country in 1991. She says, "I decided to create my own designs modeled after objects I observed in nature. This . . . forced me to invent my own compositions and techniques, which were a source of pleasure as well as anxiety!" She puts it well. That is what this book is about—creating designs, inventing compositions and techniques, and learning how to work through the design process on your own.

So much has happened in quiltmaking since I wrote *Quilts from Nature*. (See "Book List" on page 116.) Today, quilts are widely seen and appreciated, and quilters are receiving support from everyone: fabric designers and producers, equipment makers, guilds, galleries, shops, fiber-oriented publications, and an increasingly aware public. The advances and successes are directly due to the enormously focused efforts of many people—so many that you and I could hardly begin to thank them. These people have laid the groundwork for those who follow, working when it was difficult to obtain good fabric, get quilts displayed, and receive recognition. Due to their efforts, quiltmaking and fiber art is alive and vigorous.

Some mornings, as I walk into my studio, I think of the people who have done or are doing something related to what I'm doing. It's a friendly but intimidating feeling. Fortunately, I know that once I enter my own space, I am alone with my work, and whatever happens is between me and my vision. Thank heavens. Nobody looking. That's the way it has to be.

How to Use This Book

As I face that blank design wall, I am happy and grateful to be there. If the surface begins to vibrate with unexplored ideas, I am pulled into the design process. If the white space before me stays that way, I can enjoy it as a clean antidote to the clutter of living. Yet not for long — always a new fabric or a new technique will become irresistible; a room will need embellishing; or a compelling sight or scene will draw me in. I love the fluidity of this beginning.

This book is not about learning the elements and principles of design—although I will discuss them—it's about learning to be comfortable with the design process. The point of this book is that the design process itself is fluid. No matter what draws you to that design wall or what steps you follow as you work, all artists face the same challenges. As we work, possibilities are explored, sifted, and kept or discarded. Each decision we make affects all others.

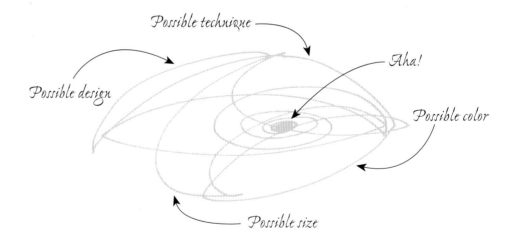

Possible technique

Aha!

Possible design

Possible color

Possible size

My feeling is that as you begin to ask yourself questions and see relationships, you gain the experience that you need to work well. You begin to see that you can also work without a step-by-step approach. You seek answers to new questions. You research, clarify, and absorb. The important thing is *you already have what you need to begin.*

This is not a textbook on design or an art book; it is something of a journal. By explaining the evolution of some of my quilts, I hope to show you how impulsive are my beginnings and how unpredictable are my results, as well as how I approach the design process. I'll lead you along, bit by bit, until we've covered many of the challenges each of us face as we work independently—the "what ifs" in design. (As I write this, I wonder if anyone really wants to hear these details. Is it like the inner workings of an emergency room? Is it better to just see the finished job? If you feel this way, skip details that intrude. Just get a feel for the overall approach.)

Many of us are most familiar with pieced quilt designs, so Part I of this book explores my design process and the issues I faced while developing a series of quilts based on shaped unit patterns. (I have provided unit patterns for three of these quilts; you can use them as a basis for developing your own compositions.) The quilts in Part II are sculptured and appliquéd. We will explore in detail my procedure for one of these quilts, "The Kelp Queen." In the last group of quilts, presented in Part III, you will see my latest ideas and design goals. Finally, in Part IV, we'll discuss the assessment process—my informal approach to the elements and principles of design.

If you are relaxed and at ease with your current design activities, your work will reflect your serenity. Don't torment yourself with change if you like where you are. My need, on the other hand, is to chase the wiggly thread just around the corner, so my process fits my need.

I encourage you to follow what interests you about the design process, benefiting from my hindsight and from what I've learned from each new quilt. I hope that this book will help you gain insight into the issues that each of us face as we work independently, as we let ourselves be open to the what ifs in design.

Are You Ready for This?

We all love a good discussion about what makes art. In contemporary art quilting, we give critical acclaim to a wide range of themes—timely, disturbing, amusing, or mysterious. (The criteria for what is award-winning varies with the times and venue.) But all these themes and motifs are "truth" for someone. My point is, simply, that you need to be secure with your own choices.

My concern is that the visual arts reveal the inner workings of the maker. Some viewers will like what you reveal; others will not. Be realistic about your growing capabilities and what you might expect from various audiences. To learn anything and to attain anything, you must risk everything, every time! But recognize that you won't always get it right. The hard part is getting used to the possibility of *really* messing up in public.

Don't consider it a waste to do a quilt you end up disliking. Focus on your vision, work through the steps you've devised for yourself, and trust that the process will ultimately yield good work.

Nobody sets out to make art; it doesn't work that way. We don't know how it happens. It is most likely to happen when you store up something that you want to say until you can't contain it any longer, and suddenly you have the impetus to produce something. "Here it is," you say. "This is what happened. This is what I made. Do you understand me? Do you respond to what I tried to say?"

The response is a separate issue. How you react to the viewer's response is controllable. Learn from it. Learn to ask questions that can be answered: "Is my piece confusing? Ho-hum? Too this? Too that? What did you see? What do you like best about what I do?"

What Do You Want to Say?

What do you want to say? I, for the moment anyway, seem to be saying, "It's not an altogether ugly world. It's still a magnificent, sparkling, amusing, amazing world." There is something about fabric that lends itself to the warm and lighthearted, and that is what draws me to quiltmaking.

I have an overwhelming sense of the grace that results from the natural shaping of objects by wind and weather—the workings of time over thousands of years. I am pulled to these objects irresistibly, hoping to mold fabric into forms that evoke this grace—sometimes delicate, sometimes grand. By oversimplifying what I see—sorting out what speaks to me—I hope to preserve a moment of beauty.

Duplicating or Copying: Attribution

One aspect of design that can be troubling is that of duplicating or "copying" another quiltmaker's work. Anyone working through a process like quiltmaking starts with a narrow range of basic tools. Our physical tools include fabric, thread, cutters, and sewing machine; our mental tools include surface-design concepts. Because we are using many of the same tools, what one person develops will very likely be developed by another, either before or after, on some unknown timetable. There is no way to prevent this, should we even wish to try.

In my own mind, I've resolved this by saying I've gotten my satisfaction from the exploration process. I'm not bothered by what happens to the design or pattern after that. But by the same token, I would be very uncomfortable if I've overlapped others' work unwittingly, calling it my own. It's getting harder to know for sure. My way of working must surely be like that of many other people. However, I'm not conversant with the working methods of other people because, when I have momentum, it's easier to find my own solution immediately than to research the solutions of others. The ability to work out such solutions comes from experience—a lifetime of attention to the details of sewing, weaving, knitting, painting, and related activities requiring hand-eye coordination and the handling of all kinds of materials.

I recommend an article in *Quilting International* magazine by Verena Rybicki: "Attribution: The Sincerest Form of Flattery," in which Rybicki assumes there will be ethical standards established in quiltmaking as our world gets more complex. (See "Book List" on page 116.)

You and Your Work

Inspirations bombard us. If you feel uninspired, you have narrowed your interests to an unusual degree. Pour over fine-art photographs, old and new. Take your camera or sketch pad outside. Look through magazines, art books, illustrated history books, and books on contemporary scientific photography. Find a computer program for quiltmakers. You may have exceedingly discerning tastes and become bored with the ordinary. If so, it's up to you to convert the ordinary into something that interests you. More often, the problem is selecting from a sea of workable ideas.

Hang on to a vision with courage and wonder.

A Place to Work

Do you have a place to go? You can spread out and work anywhere, really, when the mood strikes. But I'm coming to see more value in having a spot of your own. It's important mentally, not just for the physical convenience. You need some place where you can breathe at your own speed and work with your fabric the way you need to for a little while.

The Vision

Welcome an idea; let a vision develop. Test its possibilities. What interests you most? What seems to come to you in the most detail? Are there foreseeable difficulties? Think about how technically challenging you expect these difficulties to be and about your sense of confidence. (If you think, "I can probably figure something out for that," then proceed.)

To use an example, imagine you are a dressmaker with a client who says, "I want to be a vision in pink, and I want to be beautiful." The entire range of pinks flashes through your mind, in thousands of fabrics, falling or wrapping simply or lavishly. Is "beautiful" stately and dignified, or is it a romantic cloud of tulle and ruffles? Can either be technically accomplished on the body shape standing before you?

At some point, you need to know where you are going with this vision. You need to give it some boundaries. You need to decide on mood, color, size, contrast, design detail, and assembly technique. With a client, you could gently help her focus by asking discreet questions until you both shared the same vision. You would have a plan.

The Plan

What design will best show off this exquisite fabric? Or, what fabrics will best show off this exquisite design? You hold up fabrics, arranging and rearranging colors and textures. You toy with designs. It doesn't matter from which direction you approach this stage; the process has begun.

If you were that dressmaker, you would make a muslin sample. Or, you would pick the fabric and pattern, then you would cut—but with large seam allowances and as many options for change as possible. In quiltmaking, you usually have less money invested. You can cut out the pieces, mock up several possibilities, and assess: what design do you like, which colors are working best?

The Uncertainty

Can the dressmaker and client get through the uncertainties of the first fitting? "When it's pressed … When it's hemmed … Maybe less around the neck … You'll see …" (Anyone who has ever, like me, fitted a prom dress on her teenager will shiver at the recollection.)

This is your first test. Is your vision still holding up? Do you still want to see what happens? Or should the project be dropped? Is "revision" needed? Can a major shift in plan give you fresh interest? Do you still care about the vision? It takes vigor and enthusiasm to move beyond uncertainty. If you've got it, you have what it takes to work on your own.

The dressmaker has experience to draw on. She knows how to shape, tuck, and ease. She would not be fearful of trying a new fabric because she has experience manipulating other fabrics. She has some working tools that give her the courage to go off on tangents, redirect her efforts, revise in midstream, see what happens. She rejects some aspects that she knows cannot be done. But she says often, "I wonder what that would look like if …"

In design, you need to explore the possibilities and try things out. Can you, for example, pick out clothes from the hangers in the store and feel reasonably secure that they will look right on you? You probably know some things about yourself that help.

Sometimes we are good at narrowing down the choices to what will fit, but when it's a choice between different colors or styles, we need to "see it on." In the design process, we have nothing on the hanger, but we still need to see it on.

You can come up with what you need because you pose questions at critical moments in the design process. You say, "What do I do now? How can I do it?" This is the essence of personal creativity—to be open to anything and everything.

What do you have to draw on for courage? Take a little time to appreciate the experience you've collected in life, if not professionally, then just along the way. Any patterns or designs that you've studied have become imprinted in your brain somewhere. When you were little, did you stare at decorations, at ceiling moldings, at pictures on the wall, at illustrations in books? Add in your experience with home-decorating projects, art with children, photography, cinema, and times when you have observed, manipulated, measured, and compared. Be pleased and surprised at what you bring to the party, then watch and wonder "What if?" as your ideas take form.

Part I

Designing with Unit Patterns

The designs in this part of the book are based on a unit pattern and grid concept. The difference between these and my earlier quilts is that these designs are based on a shaped unit instead of a unit *within a block*, as below. I can repeat, twist, turn, and otherwise manipulate the shaped unit a little more freely than if I were working with a block.

Trumpeter Swans
by Joan Colvin, 1992
Bow, Washington
77" x 98"

I hope you notice that at no point have I said that working with a shaped unit rather than a block is a step forward—that simply would not be true. To me, there is no forward or backward, only "What is your current interest?"

Because I am interested in designs based on groups, flocks, and herds—which are rarely spaced uniformly—I need a unit I can grab and move about like a child with a toy farm animal. But by using shaped units, I give up the opportunity to have secondary and tertiary patterns evolve as blocks come together. This joining is fun to see and even more fun to design. So it's a loose thread for me—a place I will return to one day.

From teaching, I've learned that when I talk out loud as I work, some of your questions are answered. Your own hesitation and indecision may seem less scary if you watch me floundering and backtracking in the midst of the process. What you already do just may be the best way of all!

Pieced Quilts Based on Unit Patterns

The quilts in this section, "Arboretum Swans" and "The Brant Have Arrived," are based on a grid concept. Though they are alike in many ways, the what ifs came up differently—involving me at different times and to different degrees. You may find it useful to see the uncharted, unorganized beginning of each quilt, along with the progression of ideas. You will become comfortable with the idea that there need be no set plan of attack. So, let yourself be led along as I was, and don't worry too much about sorting it out.

Arboretum Swans—Working with Reflections

Arboretum Swans
by Joan Colvin, 1993
Bow, Washington
51½" x 51"

Developing a Vision

Swans floating amid flowers in a reflecting pond—certainly a bit of romance and a chance to use alluring, rich fabrics with abandon.

The plan is to bring together a number of swans with bodies large enough to display hand-quilting stitches, then add some flowers or shrubs to evoke the lushness of an arboretum.

Designing the Swans

I begin by designing a shape on graph paper. Using graph paper forces me to make the decisions needed to reduce shapes to manageable fabric chunks—to find essential lines and shapes.

Because I am delighted with how squares and triangles can be joined to curve into graceful neck configurations, I start with the supposition that the bodies must be in proportion to a 1½"-wide neck. On graph paper, I work to find a body shape that will rest comfortably on the surface of water and can be reversed or inverted for reflection.

By adding a triangle here and there to the swan tails, I can introduce a little variation without changing the basic pattern.

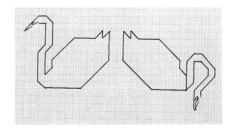

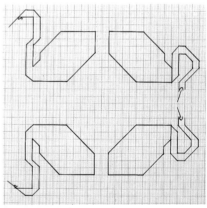

Swan –View 1
□ = 1½" finished square

17

Another simple variation fluffs the wings higher.

Wings are fluffed a little higher.

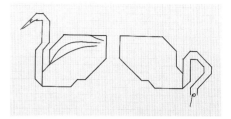

When I'm happy with the shape, I move on to developing the composition.

Developing the Composition

I cut several swan bodies, finished size, from paper to manipulate on the floor or design wall. I try different groupings to see what spaces and lines develop. I also think about the size of the finished quilt. Positioning the swans in single file would lead to a long and narrow quilt!

I use the odd-number rule, finding that groupings of three, five, or seven swans appear more graceful. I decide to include five swans. A full swan reflection can be counted as one. Since the black swan and its reflection disappear, I include one full white reflection.

Next, I make a preliminary decision on the size of the finished quilt. To do this, I determine how many 1½" squares I need to include the five swans plus the reflections, a grouping of flowers, and a little plain water at the bottom and sides. How much space should I allot to the flowers and water? If I include a massive flower garden and an extensive expanse of water, the swans will appear smaller and less important. One of the advantages of using finished-size paper units is that I can see size and scale as I develop the composition.

In this quilt, where to put the waterline or shoreline is a major design decision. (I use the term "waterline" loosely to describe the line where the real thing starts to be reflected.) As I envision it, this waterline will be almost the only horizontal movement. Above it, the flowered fabrics will be vibrant, in clear focus, and will draw the eye. Below the waterline will be the big, smooth blobs of swan and the reflected images (to be determined later when I know what is needed). Because I don't want the flowers to eclipse the swans, I settle on a waterline quite near the top. This will give me a small but powerful horizontal band of

---

Working with Different Positions

Repeating one position or pose is a safer composition than trying to use several different positions. If you are using more than one, watch carefully for integration of shapes and the relationship of lines and spaces as shapes come together.

colors—enough to set a floral scene the swans can dominate. Also, this includes some margin for error; if I need more flowers, I can add them to the top or at the waterline. If I don't need more flowers, I am free to add water fabrics that provide some movement below the waterline (such as fuzzier or softer florals, even solids).

The water area is flexible; I can use it to echo the flowers and balance the swan design or to calm or liven up the composition. I have to make a basic division of the composition without getting locked into any irreversible decisions too early in the game.

In-focus fabric and softer fabric for reflection

Testing the Plan

Now I'm ready to plunge in and test my ideas: to choose potential fabric and cut it. I look first for fabrics that suggest interesting swan bodies. I pull out all my white- and oatmeal-colored fabrics, including some with patterns and visual texture. Though I wouldn't reject a solid white or off-white, I choose several fabrics that "read" white when viewed from a few feet away. These all have some pattern to suggest texture.

I find a piece of fabric that has a wonderful tan color undulating through it, but unfortunately, there are big green and purple splotches as well.

I make a transparency of my finished-size graph-paper design for the swan body and cut it out, adding a seam allowance all around. (A cardboard or freezer-paper pattern is perfectly fine, but a photocopied transparency with potential quilting lines is best.) I position my template to get the tan shadings placed where wing lines might be quilted, but I can't do this without hitting some colored splotches as well.

What to do? I cut out an irregular shape that includes everything good and excludes the splotches, then appliqué it onto another fabric that blends with it. Now I can position the template and cut the swan body from the fabric I've constructed. I also cut squares and triangles or strips to use for necks.

Next, I need to choose floral fabrics. The nice thing about a garden is that it is easy to find floral fabrics, and it is not too taxing to make them work together.

It's satisfying to pick out a variety of floral fabrics that blend with each other. I take time to study the appearance of gardens and jungles, especially the relationship of different trees, shrubs, flowers, and ground covers. There is such a variety in size, in relationship of foliage to blooms, and in density of plantings. I try to use this in planning my quilts.

As gardens have unique character, so do fabrics. It's fun to find a fabric to express, for instance, a jungle, an English garden, a rose garden, or a group of wild flowers below a mountain. I try to establish the flavor of the garden as I choose fabric. Will it be a twelfth- or thirteenth-century walled garden with subdued tapestry fabrics or the French countryside with bright sunflower fabrics?

The concept of a garden or arboretum is so broad that there is no end to the variety of growing things that could logically (or fancifully) be present. Sometimes it's fun to find large and small flowers in a limited color scheme, adding leaves, stems, and buds from other sources. Or, construct imaginary flowers by juxtaposing petals from lots of different fabrics.

Blending florals

Before

After

As I play with the idea of sunlight and shade, I create shadow and depth by varying lights and darks.

There are dappled areas where sunlight intersperses with branches and leaves to make speckled patterns.

I linger a bit on my vision. What do I have in my scrap bag? I don't have a large collection of floral fabrics. I find that many of the flowers I like are printed on black backgrounds. Fine. I put these together, transitioning into a section where I can use florals with different-colored backgrounds. I use greenery to blend where the black backgrounds don't exactly match in color. I discard some flowers. Though printed on black backgrounds, their flavor is too somber or too contemporary for my garden.

I also look for softer floral fabrics that will do for reflections, including the reverse side of each fabric. I save some of these for reflections around the swan bodies.

Inserting a little greenery also helps blend one floral fabric with another. I don't cut up all the flowers; I can keep larger flowers intact by cutting them in modules. That is, I cut the flower fabrics into squares or rectangles based on my 1½"-square grid.

The potential floral fabrics are lying in piles on my floor, with swan bodies beside them. The total effect is fine. I like the colors, and I seem to have enough fabrics to choose from. It is time to get serious.

Because it is easiest, I work on the swan reflections first, making some fuller than others. I use some fabrics whole, uncut, for partial swan reflections. For the flower reflections, I work from the waterline, where images are less distorted, down the quilt, toward the bottom. I decide that the water at the bottom is quiet, and I choose neutral fabrics that are soothing and simple.

Working with Grids and Modules

As you work, remember that you can use any assortment of squares and triangles that will fit in a grid. You can fill in with greenery, a piece of a flower, or a shape you need. Use this chart to cut larger pieces of fabric for flowers or other elements that don't fit in a 1½" square. To cover an area with this many 1½" squares:

1½" squares	1	2	3	4	5	6	7
Cut modules*	2"	3½"	5"	6½"	8"	9½"	11"

*These measurements include ¼"-wide seam allowances.

Water is intriguing because it can be any color and any texture; it can be clear and transparent or thick with lilies, plants, and floating flowers. A reflection can be lighter or darker than the actual subject. The surface of the water can be a mirror image of the subject or a tiny rippled echo of it. Deciding how to treat the reflection is an opportunity to balance the design—to add motion or calm, to add vibrant light or shadows.

It's time to place the swan bodies on the grid. I place the necks first, using folded paper patterns because they're easier to manipulate, then place the "in-focus" (high-contrast) florals, forming the waterline. Now I can turn my attention to reflections and the water.

Creating a Reflection

If I have something floating in the water, its reflection is most precise at the waterline. In other words, I use the contrast between the fabrics and shapes to show where the swan body stops and the reflection begins.

In the illustration, triangles A and B are darker in value than the swan body.

These two triangles help define the shape of the swan. The reflection begins with triangles A1 and B1; these two triangles must mirror the angles of triangles A and B and contrast with the value. Triangles C and C1 also help define the shape of the swan body and reflection.

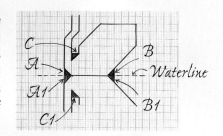

Starting a reflection so it is understandable

Assessing the Design

I stand back from my work at various stages and ask assessing questions based on my working checklist of design elements. (See "Appendix A: Elements and Principles of Design" on page 117.)

Unity of lines and shapes: Is the repetition of the swan body enough to unify the composition? Are there messy places? I focus on the flowers and water around the swan necks and between their bodies. I checked out negative space with the paper pieces—designing the neck shapes so almost any juxtapositioning would be pleasant enough. Now I'm checking to see if the reflections added something unexpected.

Visual movement: The eye winds around in the light necks and bodies. Will it come in at the top left if I have some white flowers there? Then it should go through the swans and out the bottom at the reflected neck. But it will come back in and start over, I hope, at the reflection of the bottom swan's body.

Spatial relationships: Looking at the relationship of lines and spaces, I think that the swans, all the same size, are calming. I hope the quilting lines and the breakup of reflections will keep them from being boring. Are there enough flowers? How about the final size of the quilt? Is it balanced? Does it need more on the top or bottom? I like that the swan bodies could touch the border, as I now have it on the grid, and doing that moves all the large white spaces a little off-center to the left.

Contrast: My swans are very light against the mediums and darks. I like the black floral with white flowers; it sets the tone for the quilt. I've added the black swan to carry on the darks and to calm the piece (a white swan would have rounded out the swans into a huge petallike clump, taking over the whole space).

This is what I see when I squint:

Seems OK to me.

Viewing distance: This piece will be nice from any distance. Flowers are usually no problem because they are interesting in colorful banks and drifts as well as in a bouquet. The textured swan fabrics look solid white from a distance; they become more interesting as you move closer.

Assembling and Finishing

In general, I piece the quilt top in horizontal or vertical rows. To avoid inset seams, I add triangles of water fabric to convert necks and bodies to rectangles. (Some people find it easier to assemble the floral backgrounds, then appliqué the swan necks.)

For the swan beaks, I try to find printed fabrics that include the pink-orange as well as the black of a swan beak, or I construct the fabric I need. I use a transparent template (a photocopy on a transparency) to help determine where I should cut each beak. I appliqué the swan beaks before quilting.

I quilt inside the swan bodies, around the flowers (quilting inside them sometimes), and in horizontal lines spreading across the water.

As for the border, my "stopper" (the dark narrow inner border) holds the piece together without being too noticeable. I think the light band leads into the swans. This is a traditional-looking frame for a sort of romantic, old-fashioned picture.

Afterword

If you want to modify my unit pattern or create your own, study photographs of these stately birds. Look at how the wings are connected and the positions the neck can assume. Store information for shading, color, and quilting lines. Think and feel *swan*. Then include your own observations in the unit pattern.

It is a delight to see what students do with my designs. During a class discussion, I suggested, among other things, that my waterline wasn't sufficiently distinct. With that in mind and lots of thoughtful work, Pat Goffette created a spectacular version of this quilt. She combined richly interwoven flowers, careful reflections, and an inspired fabric selection for an elegant composition.

The unit pattern for "Arboretum Swans" appears on pages 119–21.

Shadow Lake
by Pat Goffette, 1994
Edmonds, Washington
65" x 65"

The Brant Have Arrived—Creating Directional Flow

The Brant Have Arrived
by Joan Colvin, 1993
Bow, Washington
60½" x 57½"

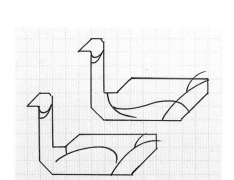

Developing a Vision

It's a nice sight when these small, dark geese arrive in a flurry on Puget Sound. As they dip into the waves to eat eel grass, their lovely lacelike neck markings give them an air of having dressed for the affair.

What strikes me is the distinctive side marking this bird has, as well as his lace necklace. Both define the species. Also, I like the idea of high contrast—black and white against a medium gray for water.

I would like to do an assortment of these geese floating in the water. It's a simple concept. The fun will be in positioning the bodies, playing with color, and experimenting with values. I envision this quilt as a giant grid, just like "Arboretum Swans," to be filled in with black brant, reflections, or water.

Designing the Geese

I have graph paper, so I try a quick, small sketch to get going.

I make a larger version, sticking to the 1½" finished square for the neck width. The actual size of the finished body will be roughly 4½" x 13½". In other words, each brant will be 13½" long, and the top of its back will be 4½" above the waterline. That's almost life-size. This may be fine, but how big will the quilt be? I make fifteen photocopies, which should be enough for birds of this size.

☐ = 1½" finished square

Developing the Composition

How many brant in the flock? I see hundreds, crowded together, changing positions constantly. This is where I find working with unit patterns most exhilarating; there are so many pleasant possibilities. I can play with lining up the angles of the bodies, touching them, stacking them, and curving the necks.

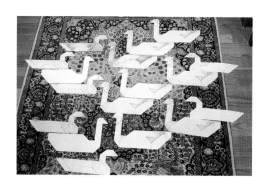

I found another bird shape to add flavor to the group. The slightly different neck position complements the first:

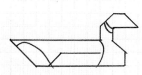

At this point, I expect to make six to eight birds in each position, and I also expect to use the two graph-paper units as drawn. I plan three birds across (14" x 3 = 42"), which puts the quilt in the range of four feet square. That's fine.

Testing the Plan

It's best to mock up a few birds on the design wall to see what values are needed. I can't determine the relationship of lights and darks or what patterns will emerge from repetition by looking at just one bird. I could add an intermediate step, planning value on graph paper or on a computer program (if I had one), but with very little effort, I can work with real fabric. I prefer this approach because:

- § I have precut lights and darks from other projects.
- § The pattern is very simple and easy to mock up. Changes can be made immediately, directly on the design wall.
- § If I produce any I like, assembling the bird is simple. I'll get the beginnings of color and value relationships—enough to know how to formulate additional birds. So, I'll make some birds on the design wall.

It's pleasant to look at fabric in terms of its directional pattern, then turn little triangles to look like feathers.

Black may be the absence of color, but it's a nice surface for the reflection of lots of colors. The black seems to blend into brown on these brant—they almost have a rusty waterline! Soon I have a sense that these birds will work. The units are large enough to display fabric nicely, and even the rather monochromatic color scheme holds my attention.

Before I am too committed to color, however, and certainly before I spend much time refining the details of each bird, I must see what I have for the water.

These I used.

These I did not use.

As I go through my fabric, I am struck by several unusual pieces:

- ♪ A khaki green and inky blue hand-dyed blend
- ♪ A pale gray and white that makes me think of whitecaps
- ♪ A rose sprayed with gray for a wrinkled texture
- ♪ A pair of acid-washed jeans from Paris that looks rosy tan in places

I try a combination of the last three:

Spots and speckles dot the jeans, which may explain why they were marked down to ten dollars, but the specks blend into the gray and white fabric. And the rosy tan is nice near the rosy gray. I find usable pieces of the jeans and pin them to the design wall, interspersing some of the other possible water fabrics. Nice. (Is the denim too thick and heavy to hand quilt? I think not. I quilt a small piece successfully.)

So, I make a tentative decision. I can include a bit of rose in the bird bodies. Some golden brown, blending into black, will be warm and lend some bite to the rose. I think rose and gray can look a little cold without some peach, yellow, or brown nearby.

Creating Light, Color, and Reflection in Water

Even in photos taken on the same day, there is variation in water color. Choosing fabric for water without any thought is sad—a missed opportunity for your own pleasure and that of your viewers.

Any scene must begin with some sense of the light. Close your eyes and remember or imagine what happens in the earliest dawn and as the sun slowly rises. Is it going to be a clear day or an overcast day? What season is it? How does the light affect the colors of the water and birds? Imagine the light at noon, in the late afternoon, at sunset, by moonlight. After this mental exercise, treat yourself to a day at the museum, in the park, in the galleries, or in the bookstore. Now you are open and ready to absorb details to enrich your perceptions of color and light.

So, is the water blue or green? Sometimes. Sometimes it's pink, orange, teal, and dark brown. You can justify the use of any color you like! Simply remember that both water and objects will reflect the color or colors you choose. If your sunset is lavender, there is bound to be some lavender in the water, in the birds, and in the birds' reflections.

Start with a simple color concept. Use color to unify your composition and establish a mood.

My flock is beginning to take shape on the fleece.

I plan to use the white tails and bird reflections to draw the flock together—that is, to tighten up my design so I have directional flow. I hope to bring the viewer's eyes diagonally down, in, and around to join the whitecaps created by the pale gray and white fabric. The wispy reflections of the tails will soften the diagonal lines.

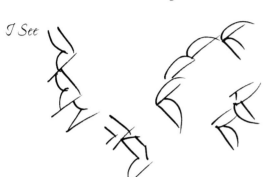

Looking again at my interim working photo, I don't think there is any way for the viewer's eyes to get in at the top. The white crescent of fleece at the top of this photo gives me an idea that a bit of wave or light at the top right would help.

The dark necks and bodies are setting up a flow of their own. From the top outer edges, they seem to converge at a point in the lower center. Maybe I can take advantage of that to gently move into darker water—a larger area of plain, dark water would offset the larger area of whitecap. This might be the perfect place to introduce the first water fabric I liked—the khaki green and inky blue blend. It might add richness and dimension. It's certainly not garish in any way; dark and muddy, actually.

When I squint, I see these darks:

The light and dark areas seem fine—just a natural sweep.

Once I have chosen a fabric, I am inclined to use it more than once. I may use a cluster of it in one place, then use dots and dabs throughout the quilt. Or, I may use it in part of the unit pattern in one area, then use it in other parts elsewhere. I may use ten to twenty other fabrics in this same way—weaving them throughout and probably into unrelated subjects or areas.

Traveling Across the Surface of the Composition

By repeating a particular fabric, I can guide the viewer's eye across the surface of the composition. There are many ways to guide the viewer's eye—repeating color, texture, scale, or motif. This basic concept is used by all surface designers. For example, you can travel with a line:

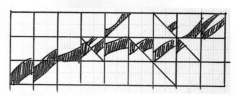

How you position the triangle template over the fabric "line" before cutting and how you choose to arrange the resulting triangles determine the movement.

Notice in the illustration that my lines do not quite meet. This irregularity is how I get the looseness and power of a brush stroke or natural line. If you want mathematical purity or an engineered look, the lines must meet exactly, like assembling plastic pipe.

Now I can get back to working on my bird bodies. I need to focus on value, texture, and blending. Before me is a paper copy of a brant on which I must mark light, medium, and dark values.

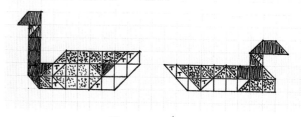

Pattern values

My brant photograph shows that certain areas must be light or dark. However, I can use a softening, transitional fabric in many places. I mark especially critical light/dark feather transitions with a T.

The lace collar at the base of each brant head needs a little dark at the top of the triangle to unite it with the dark head. Within each bird, there can be enormous variation in texture and color as long as the defining values are maintained. I do not always adhere to my diagram or unit pattern. I let the fabric guide me, changing squares to triangles to blend different fabrics, or turning triangles to position the fabric pattern in a way that suggests the direction of feather growth.

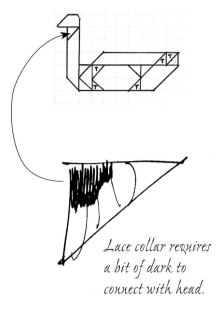

Lace collar requires a bit of dark to connect with head.

The rest of the water is now a blend of rosy tan, green, inky blue, and white. As I choose which of these to use where, I make some small decisions:

- § Does this area need a calm, quiet contrast to the heavily pieced, active birds and reflections? I find several places where I feel better with large modules of uncut, unseamed water fabric.
- § Does this area need a transition between two or more different colors of water? In grid-based quilts, I often use triangles to move from one color to another or to integrate larger modules into the grid. (This is like blending big, chunky daubs of paint with a large brush.) I choose fabrics with some of the colors in the adjoining fabrics for the triangles. Adding other fabrics in related colors can help.

Assembling and Finishing

As in my other grid-based quilts, I try to fill out my unit shapes into manageable chunks before assembly. To make the brant look more lifelike, I tuck under the corner of each head and appliqué the curve.

I decide not to appliqué the beaks. Brant beaks are small and black. Highlighting them with appliqué serves no identifying purpose. (Also, my brant heads are so black that the little beaks would hardly show.)

I quilt around the brant to offset them, softening body lines. Quilting the water is easier than usual because I can follow the printed or etched textures within the fabric. This is no coincidence; I had "seen" quilting lines when choosing the water fabric.

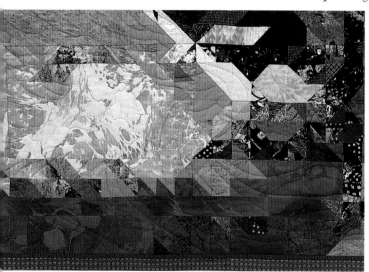

I have no clear plan for the border. I often try a stopper of unrelated color and find I can use more formal repetitive prints in the border or a fabric that has been brought along from the beginning but not yet used. One medium purple-green qualifies. A neutral tan quietly extends the edges.

Afterword

I am comfortable with this quilt, and I get pleasure from how the process worked from beginning to end. I could have improved details in the composition, but I got the flavor of my vision without much effort.

The unit pattern for "The Brant Have Arrived" appears on pages 122–25.

Pieced and Appliquéd Quilts
Based on Unit Patterns

The next two quilts are a bit different. Though the unit or object is pieced or designed to be pieced, for varying reasons, I did not use a complete grid format to incorporate the units into a pieced background. But the process is generally the same. In "Faced with Foxes," I focused on mood and flavor. "Tundra Swans" is a good example of a basic design that could be implemented in a variety of different ways.

Faced with Foxes—Creating Character, Mood, and Flavor

Faced with Foxes
by Joan Colvin, 1994
Bow, Washington
59" x 61½"

Developing a Vision

Separate events come together: a flood of fox pictures in *National Geographic*, in catalogs, and in Christmas cards; a growing collection of red ocher fabrics (over time, my favorite color); and a gift from a friend: a piece of cotton drapery fabric with large, sweeping brush strokes.

Designing the Foxes

I found myself thinking of red foxes, lots of them. What could they be doing? Walking home. Curling up in their dens. How would you do that in fabric? I try to sketch a curled-up fox in its den.

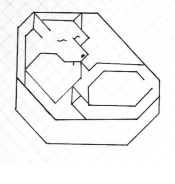

I try sketching another with a slightly different shape.

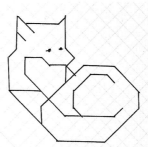

What about one coming into the den?

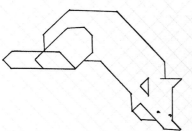

What if I put these two together?

When I squint at this design, it looks like two interlocking shrimp. I don't know. I'll assume I can get a good shape with more work.

Can I get fur from fabric? Can I get a face? Better play with it right now before I fall in love with a bad idea.

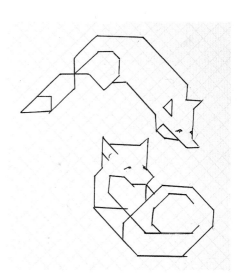

Here is a little fox with a white vest and the smiley face of the catalog. What do I think? I think it looks like a tea cozy. And it's too syrupy.

Maybe I'm just not in the mood. No, the trouble is the face looks like preprinted doll's-head fabric, and the flowered fabrics are, as a result, too cute. I want a more serious approach. That front ruff . . . it's too crisp and could be mistaken for a beard. So back to the face; use a different fabric and less detail? This face is pleasant enough, but when I stand back a few feet, there's no strength, no definition.

Try opening the eyes and getting rid of the weak chin line. Better.

What do I want to see from a midviewing distance? Or what can I expect to see? I want to see large eyes and a black nose. So try again.

This could work. This fox doesn't look sweet or dreamy. He's alert and his face is sufficiently defined to read "fox" from midviewing distance.

So what now? Is it possible to put such a face on a body? Here is a point to ponder. It's a lot of trouble to convert an animal into a believable, graceful pieced pattern. It would be easy to do a pen-and-ink drawing or get out my paints and do a watercolor. I could even do a lifelike fabric painting. What is possessing me to push and squeeze this design onto graph paper? The grid approach is really too rigid for the vibrancy and fluidity of a beautiful fox.

I should pull back here, but I don't. Somehow the treasure hunt for perfect fabrics and the neatness of repetition in a grid pulls me toward this concept.

Testing the Plan

I'm looking for shades of red ocher in my less structured fabrics—no flowers, no prints. Except I'm drawn back to the furry look of a popular cat print. I can use it by carefully placing my fox eyes and nose to get lighter areas under the muzzle. Small squares and triangles of it will simulate the lighter underbelly and tip of the tail.

I manipulate these pieces until I have a believable body position—a crouch that doesn't require legs. During this manipulation process, I find that 2" finished squares will fit the head size I've been working on.

Now that I'm getting some sense of this design, I find hand-dyed fabrics with striations and textures that provide a certain fluidity. The facial expression looks a little different when drawn on different fabrics. (I use a template to find the best position on the fabric and mark dots at key points to guide my lines. I hand draw each face, using a permanent Micron Pigma marking pen.)

The faces must somehow be joined to pieced bodies. I am not able to get strength from the expression if I force the face to fit some configuration of squares and/or triangles. It seems that I must tip the head a bit and appliqué it onto the shoulders. I'll decide how to make and attach the ears when I join the head and the body.

How about foxes in their dens? I suddenly see that without a beard, the tea cozy is curled up, looking back over her shoulder at me.

Partially what I'm doing, I think, is trying to say, swiftly, simply, "Here is a fox made out of a couple of quick shapes. How can that be?"

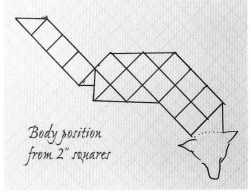

Body position from 2" squares

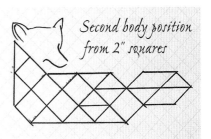

Second body position from 2" squares

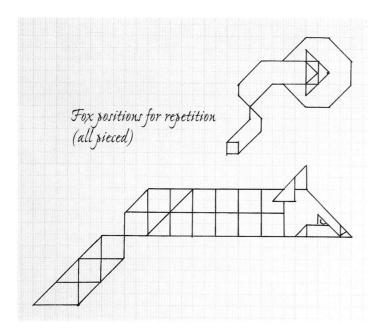

Fox positions for repetition (all pieced)

Developing the Composition

Stop to think a bit about character, mood, and flavor. What do I have here? Where am I going with the background and setting? My early impulse was to repeat the unit, as I've done before, but I'd need to build a purer fox unit and stick to squares that behave (unlike the free-form head I've drawn). These two quick designs show what I mean; they would be fun for children's quilts.

But clearly, I'm not going in that direction. Having been "drawn in" by the faces, I'm trying for a little more anatomical accuracy. The hand-dyed, red ocher fabric gives the fox bodies a painted look that is as close as I can come to the flowing feeling I want.

I know what effect I am looking for when I sort through fabric for backgrounds. The fox bodies seem to nestle into the big brush-stroke tan-and-gray fabric. Suddenly there are rocks and underbrush for the foxes to creep through. They are coming out of the woods. To what? Why?

What if I stopped here? Just used the upper right area as a complete composition? It's not bad.

I still have the sense that these foxes are coming home to curl up in their dens. I find several fabrics with a warm, dark underground feeling and nestle a slightly revised reclining fox into them. Where I can, I use darker reds for the fox. (I'm worried that not much light would be shining down into the den. Oh, for heaven's sake. This is just for fun, not for a scientific journal.) Looking at what I have so far, I also need some lighter fur—some salmon peach to lead back up to the lighter-furred foxes.

I need to tie the dens together with forest floor, grasses, sticks, and flowers; find these fabrics. What should I be cutting, though? I don't want to cut the tan-gray rocks, nor do I want to cut the dark, denlike fabric. Both stand on their own as large-patterned paintings. I will appliqué pieced objects onto them then. This way, I can position the foxes to best show off the fabric.

Since I'm planning to piece all the fox bodies, I'd better piece at least part of the forest floor. The repetition of technique will help weave this composition together. I think the wide brush strokes in the tan-gray drapery fabric will help blend the background with the pieced fox bodies and pieced forest floor.

I'm thinking of this as a forest, but there are no trees yet. There is, however, a real need for dark trees to balance the dark dens. Wait—I could lighten the dens and everything could become snowy. I've let myself get stuck enjoying the rich dark fabrics. *What if I change my approach? It might well be fabulous—snowy whites and foxes with fur getting snowy white as you come forward in the scene.* If I keep the dark dens, I'll need to weave in some dark trees toward the top of the scene and include some gray trees to tie in the rocky fabric, giving the illusion of distance in the upper right area. (Everything looks slightly gray and misty in the distance.) That works!

Should the trees be appliquéd at random? Should they be pieced? Either would work, but I think I'll get a natural, softer effect and have more flexibility if I appliqué the trees onto the rocky background.

Sometimes, my assembly techniques emerge from the fabrics I use and the flavor of the composition.

Forming Trees

When you fold fabric to audition for trees, surprises emerge. Circles become knots in the tree bark. A formally repeated pattern becomes natural-looking markings.

I always cut way too many strips of tree fabric, but you never really know which fabrics will be most effective. It's more natural and lifelike to cut freely across the fabric, forming tree trunks that reflect the eccentricities of nature. I assemble the strips into taller trees by stitching them together in progressive sizes.

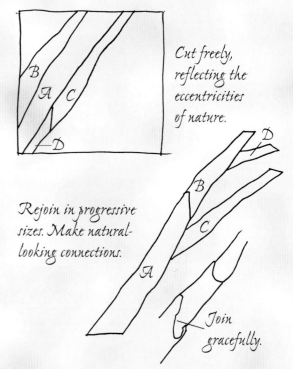

Cut freely, reflecting the eccentricities of nature.

Rejoin in progressive sizes. Make natural-looking connections.

Join gracefully.

Standing back, I'm glad to see that though all the foxes are the same size, the three foxes in the upper right area look smaller than those in the foreground because they are lighter and behind trees.

For some reason, I make sure the foxes are aligned with the grid (on-point in this quilt) before I appliqué. It seems the right thing to do. Habit dies hard!

The composition appears complete, though I need to work on graceful transitions to integrate the grass and rock. Refining positions, colors, textures, and values will continue for a while, in any case.

Assembling and Finishing

The little fungus growth on the stump—these things just happen as you get into the mood of your work. I could never plan that.

Ears on the foxes—a bit messy but not possible to ignore. I've been putting this off, edging into it, knowing I'd need to deal with it. In fact, this tiny aspect almost stopped me at the outset as I tried to integrate my heads with the little pieced bodies. Sculpting, stealing printed cats' ears, sketching my own—nothing looks right. As I stare at fox pictures, those ears, so alert, just poke out. That's it— Prairie Points!

A Prairie Point looks crisp, and I can mold it to the head. Using lighter fabrics for the inside of the ears will help say "fox." I make this decision at some cost because, in my mind, Prairie Points evoke a somewhat different image.

I have come dangerously close to "sentimental" with this work, but I think these foxes have a look that is beyond sweet—they dare you to come closer or to disturb them further. One more second and they will have scrambled to safety, out of view. Perhaps I've done too much work for a moment of amused response. And perhaps I've created once again, not serious art, but whimsy.

Making Prairie-Point Ears

For each ear, you need 1 strip of fabric, 2½" x 5", for the dark fur, and 1 strip of fabric, 2" x 5", for the light fur.

1. Place the 2 strips with right sides together. Using a ¼"-wide seam allowance, stitch down one long side.

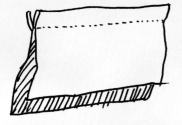

2. Open and finger-press the strips so ¼" of the dark fur shows. The bottom edges of the strips should be even.

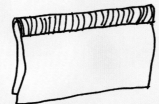

3. Fold the ends of the strips over at a 45° angle.

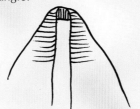

4. Fold the ends back about halfway so you can see more light fur.

5. Slip the ear under the head and squeeze, shape, and turn a bit until you are happy with the way it looks. Pinching to keep the shape, remove the ear and stitch across the bottom.
6. Trim the bottom ¼" from your stitching, then reinsert the ear and appliqué the fox head over it.

Hand quilting would hardly be noticeable in the activity set up by the fabric and the design, so I use machine quilting to set off the trees and the foxes. My quilting lines curve through the bodies. I can use almost any undulating line to hold down the grasses and rocks. I tend to follow the patterns in the fabric.

While I'm quilting, I think about borders. But I make no decision until the last minute. A border is my safety device. I am living with the current shape of my design as I quilt, but I am mentally cropping it, assessing the dimensions. In this case, putting a wide, straight band next to an undulating tree constricts the tree. So a wide frame is out. I need the feeling of outdoor expanse. I could use the tan-gray fabric to extend the top border skyward, but I haven't a scrap of it left. If I bring my stopper down, using the first few inches of the top as the frame, I could improvise a border on the sides with blended fabrics. This concept pleases me. Using a stopper alone as a frame will give the effect I want: open but controlled in the same way we peer through the viewfinder of a camera. The dark stopper also pulls in the bottom right corner and neatens the whole thing without arresting the action.

Afterword

This quilt did provoke some later discussion. It was popular in the sense I'd hoped: "Look what can be done with a few squares and triangles!" But the free treatment of the trees and background apparently promised something more serious, and some considered the faces to be cartoonlike and off-flavor for that reason.

My sense of being too close to sentimental with this work was justified. Since I decided that I couldn't do serious art with these few components, I adjusted to whimsy. My options would have been to change the foxes entirely or to eliminate them.

See how important mood and flavor become? Mixtures of fabrics and moods can result in something splendid. Juxtaposing all sorts of things is what art is all about, isn't it? But it's a good idea to keep avenues of escape open. Use rules to stabilize and help, not to fetter. (Did I make my "fox rules" too rigid?) The more aware I am of possibilities, the richer my choices. I work until a point of view becomes clear. But it may be confusing to the viewer if I'm not clear what mood I am conveying.

In literature, mixtures sometimes work brilliantly and sometimes leave the reader confused and disappointed, wondering why it wasn't possible to identify with the characters or get into their problems. No author confuses his or her reader on purpose. No visual artist does either. Here is one more reason to remember to ask, "What am I really trying to say?"

A sample face shape is at right. You can work from the fox bodies in this section or use your imagination.

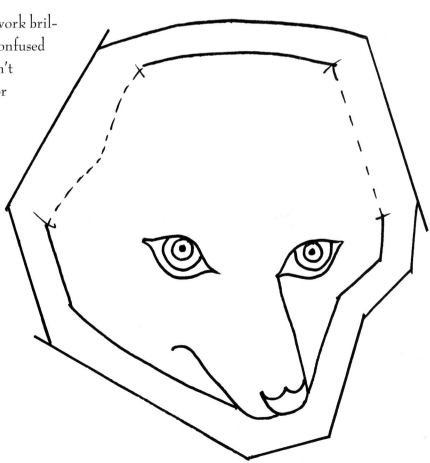

Tundra Swans—Implementing a Clear Vision

Tundra Swans
by Joan Colvin, 1994
Bow, Washington
49" x 49"

Developing a Vision

I had seen a magazine photo of tundra swans. Backlit with gold from a late afternoon sun, the masses of purple swans stood close together on a shore. This image stuck in my memory.

In a painting, it's easy to create rims of light behind an object. Paint the background with light, then paint dark birds, leaving bits and pieces of the light flowing through untouched. Or, paint a line of bright color around the edges of the image.

I could use fabric to create a double image—a dark image over a light image. What about yellow piping?

The piping looks too tight, too military, and it's too hard to apply gracefully. Where does the piping start, where does it stop?

What else would work? Well, if I use warm colors to create a light-filled beach and dark colors for the swans, then I should get a silhouetted look—the effect of backlighting. I'll go with this idea.

What if I'd been freer and less literal with my lighting concept? I could have made light swan images that were not always the same color light or not always exactly behind the positive image. A whole secondary matrix of light swans would have developed in the background. The effect would have been more graphic design than photorealism. Or, what if I'd thought of using heavy machine embroidery around the edges of the birds?

Crayonlike fabric

Testing the Plan

Try purplish fabrics on warm golds and oranges. I have a great many lavender fabrics. Should I move into lavender mixes with other colors? Large-scale lavender prints are tempting. But what makes a silhouette? I am looking into the light, and the dazzle of it leaves me unable to pick out details on the dark surface. This eliminates high-contrast prints. I can use large-scale prints, but I want prints that are "fuzzy" and low contrast. What value should I use? Well, I don't care at this point. In reality, the birds are gray to white and, against the sun, could be almost black. So don't worry, use all values for now.

I pull out all sorts of lavenders. One especially attracts me—a fuzzy, large-scale print fabric in lavender-gray, tan, teal, and black. The print reminds me of a crayon drawing and may evoke the idea of feathers.

Could I tie in this fabric with a crayonlike or chalklike drawing? I don't have fabric crayons at hand, but I do have several colors of Fabric Mate™ pens: black, gray, yellow ocher, and something called "suede." On a piece of muslin, I play with sketching swans. I use suede, which turns out to be sort of mauve.

I backlight the swans with the yellow ocher. Nice.

That loosely filled-in body, tiny as it is (about 2″ across), could possibly be the link with this crayonlike fabric. I have been wanting to use these pens to enhance fabric in a quilt. What if I use the best of these little sketches in a distant landscape, then use larger birds in the foreground?

This was a major decision that narrowed my options considerably. The mood and colors of my sketch dictated lots of later decisions (choice of fabrics, choice of colors, variations in size, realistic painting versus graphic design). Had I eliminated the sketch, I could have used a traditional block in any size, using any technique. When I decided to use my realistic sketch, I limited my design to a natural, more realistic scene. (That's the way my mind was working. Of course, many people successfully juxtapose natural imagery with geometric shapes.)

Refine the fabrics selected for swan bodies. Get some of that suede color. Get some that blend with the crayonlike fabric. Look for a fabric to use for a distant beachlike horizon that blends with the muslin sketch.

Funny, when you start looking for specific things, you find them. The treasure hunt through what I have is such fun. Not only do I look at the whole piece of fabric (holding my little sketches against each piece for match or blend), I look for tiny parts of good color in multicolored, patterned pieces.

Fabrics I'd forgotten jump out. Fabrics I'd mentally discarded turn out to be surprisingly effective, at least at close range with my head in the fabric closet. So I pull out a pile on the floor and make some preliminary choices as I see how these blend with the warm beach tones and lavenders I've already chosen. At this point, the more vivid purples are discarded in favor of the mauves and tan pink/purples.

But the real treasure, the "find," is a small slice of watery-looking decorator fabric with a dark stem design. When I turn this fabric sideways, I see a horizon line that suggests a reflection of the sky in water—not accurately, but enough to give the flavor. Ho, ho! This fabric has an oatmeal-colored background that will tie in with the muslin. Now I'm irresistibly pulled toward the little sketch.

I need to look closely at the color effect of this sky from a distance, now that it has become my one sure fabric. Can I still use my original color scheme? Yes, because as I stand back, the pinks and tans blend into lavender. And the diffuse brush strokes can be nudged in any color direction by means of applied color. (Sometimes I use pastel pencil, pens, or paint to add a bit of color.)

So, enough fabric surrounds me. I'll find what I need from this pile.

The strip of horizon fabric, which I've constructed to be sure the concept works, lies across my design wall. The strip is 48" wide. That's all I have. I could extend it, of course, by integrating other fabrics, but let's say 48" will do for now. It is easiest.

I use pastels to enhance slightly when color doesn't quite suit me.

I am bothered a bit by the vertical seam lines. Am I bothered enough to junk this idea? Lots of quiltmakers I admire might stop here. When I stand back a few feet, I can't see the seams. But I know they are there. I decide that if the design is interesting and strong, the seams will not intrude.

Has stopping to notice the seams and to think through the implications dampened my excitement? That's the issue for me. Do I still want to see what happens with this piece of fabric, or have alternate ideas begun to replace the original one? I need to think about this.

Pin the cutout sketch to the strip of horizon. Actually, I love it. Have to see what happens. (This quilt will be for me; I won't even show it to anybody.)

Designing the Swans

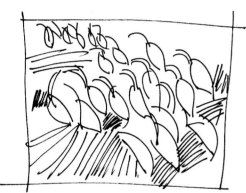

I need to design a unit that will fit in my setting. What size and shape for the basic swans? I want my design a little smaller than usual because I envision a crowd of birds. The easy way is to design a unit pattern based on a finished 1" square instead of a 1½" square. I'll start there, sketching on graph paper.

What if I'd chosen to appliqué a free-form bird? This could be a lovely design, with realistic shapes in several positions, overlapped. It might have been best of all with the sketches. Did I miss an opportunity? Another loose thread.

Referring to my original color sketches, I make some shapes on graph paper that combine the body positions. The body that results is diamond shaped.

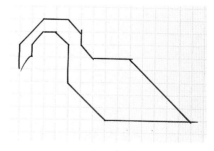

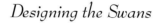 = 1½" finished square

The necks, though, can do anything. The idea of using the necks for a repetitive "loop" design intrigues me.

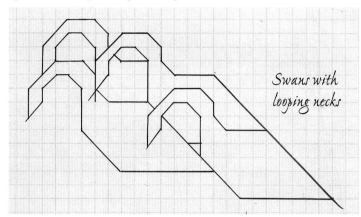

Swans with looping necks

I duplicate my graph-paper pattern, which is finished size, and cut out seven or eight swans to manipulate. I want to see what connections I can make and look for unpleasant negative space.

There are so many positions from which to choose. What if I choose these? The design effect could be totally different with upright birds. Or, I could combine left and right facing birds or upright and level ones.

Developing the Composition

To get the effect of my design fast, I cut this shape out of the crayonlike fabric, which I'm guessing will look better whole, not pieced. Also, I cut a shape from a pinkish tan fabric. I have two swans to place on the design wall. Mentally, I fill in the space between my horizon and foreground with lots and lots of lavender swans. The pinkish tan fabric ties in the horizon fabric. I will need to use more of this color.

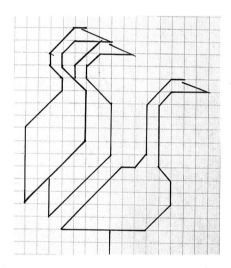

I'm restless to see the effect of lots of birds. Think I'll skip the piecing process for the moment. I have several fabrics with subtle striations and textures that might work uncut. I use a transparent template to position those textures in the body, letting shadings work for me to become or suggest feathers or wing lines. The template is great fun, and I cut out lots of swans, placing them on the design wall in what starts out as a uniform pattern but becomes a bit haphazard. (Don't want to cover up that wing texture, so move him out, forward. That one is plain; can go in the back. This fabric has to be next to that....)

Standing back to assess, I see the necks loop nicely. Almost any position is satisfactory. I can play with positions later on. What if I just skip the piecing and appliqué these uncut shapes directly onto the background?

What is the advantage of piecing? Piecing can give the design a rich, faceted look. That's not essential here because the gentle brush-stroke pattern of the horizon fabric establishes a watercolor mood. And that large-scale, crayonlike fabric provides the same richness that piecing would, but is less angular. Piecing the calmer, one-color birds needed to balance the crayonlike fabric would be a waste of time. And as I visualize it, the background is more likely to be curves than lines of color (or maybe just solid).

There are advantages to whole-cloth swans. It's much easier to overlap them in a crowded group, and I could get a softer look with more obvious quilting lines. This softer look will emphasize the watery, sketchy mood.

What if I piece these swans, putting them in a different scene? This is a nice design that could become richly feathered, with careful attention to directional fabrics that suggest these curving lines. Then the background could be linear, with diagonal slashes to change color or indicate sedges or reefs. The birds could be spaced a bit farther apart or clumped for variety, and the necks could vary in position. There would be no small or distant birds. I think this would be gorgeous.

Patterns for pieced swans

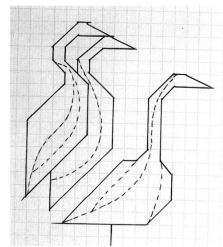

Quilting lines

Another idea pops up. Maybe a medium-size bird would work. (I'm planning to appliqué anyway.) A cluster of these would provide a transition from background to foreground, as well as a transition from my sketch to the commercial fabrics. After making a pattern one-third the size of the original, I cut several from the pinkish tan fabric and one from a plain mauve fabric, which I enhance with the suede Fabric Mate pen.

Assessing the addition of these medium-size swans, I am pleased to see that they lend credibility to the scene. My habit is to repeat a unit of the same size, even though size is supposed to decrease with distance. I can push this same-size concept pretty far by using lighter values and less detail. But in a scene where objects recede into the distance, going to an intermediate size makes sense.

So where am I? What am I trying to do at this point? I have the horizon and the flock (in various sizes, in various shades of lavender, in various textures). That fits my original vision. How to finish it off?

Testing the Plan

I'd planned a gold background, but now I have a lighter beige (from the sketch and strip of horizon) to deal with. Maybe I'll be less dramatic and just try for warm colors flowing out from this beige.

I return to the fabrics I originally pulled out. One fabric has a little sweep of suede color that resembles a bird head. To match it up with a medium-size neck is irresistible.

Using fabrics that shade from light gold to red ocher, I lay in strips and swatches behind the swans. Since I'm working on a beach scene, I can use tide pools for soft reflections. A shimmery gold fabric, used as a reflection for a plain gold fabric, adds richness and glow. In the same way, a pink-and-rust marbled fabric softens the intensity of a red ocher fabric. (Maybe too much? But I want to use it. How often do you get a chance to use those colors?)

How high will this piece be? I guess this question is like "How much is enough?" When you get tired? When you've said it all? When you've used it up? When you can't lift it?

My width seems fine. I use the fabrics I have, one or sometimes two swans of each as the mood strikes. The composition has become almost square, which appeals to me. To finish off the bottom, do I introduce different swan fabrics or more of some I've used?

Maybe I should *piece* one gorgeous swan for the foreground. No, I've already rejected that as being too angular for the softer concept.

Do I use some watery fabrics for reflections, thus doing something different at the bottom? Adding some unstructured reflections might smooth down the bottom, bringing the flock to a halt and continuing the idea of reflection started by my pink/red ocher puddle on the right side. I know I have introduced a sort of choppiness over there, but I think a dark, plain bird could balance that.

What if I had made more birds and/or added length to the quilt? I could have focused on value. If I had enlarged the far right clump of medium-value birds and extended them down across the left, clumped some light-value birds on the left, and placed darker-value birds across the foreground, the piece might have made a purer, stronger statement.

Assessing the Design

Stand back and look. I've been squinting since I started this quilt. But this is almost the last chance to rearrange and change. I do change some things.

When I squint, I see the light and dark values like this:

There is a flow that doesn't displease me. My eyes start in a light area where the high-contrast, medium-size birds are standing at the water's edge, continue up to the sketch, then follow the colors toward the bottom right. I am fooled into thinking the bottom swans are shaped as freely as those in the sketch. They seem more varied in position than I know they really are.

How should this composition be framed or cropped? I adjust the bottom up a bit and the right side over, to tighten up the composition. I don't need full reflections of the bottom swans, but I do need the neck of the dark one to pull the viewer's eyes back up into the picture. The inaccurate neck reflection of the light bird to its immediate left helps pull the choppy water down around to the front.

I quickly sort through my working checklist of design elements. (See "Appendix A: Elements and Principles of Design" on page 117.)

- **Unity of lines and shapes:** The repeated swans create unity.
- **Visual movement:** I followed the flow of lines, shapes, and colors and decided it was fine.
- **Contrast:** Using light to set a mood was the starting point of my idea. Somewhere I lost the original impact of light rims on each bird. I wonder why? Maybe the horizon fabric with the beige in it looked more like bright daylight than intense setting sun. I didn't feel the need for dramatic highlighting; that idea was not lost, simply diluted. The larger shapes of red-orange beach served the same purpose.
- **Spatial relationships:** I used three sizes for realism and drama, but the same shape for a calming effect.
- **Viewing distance:** This quilt is going to be best from many feet away, since the total composition makes sense. Up close, one might wonder at certain color choices. (I'm not a teal, pink, and orange fan myself. At a distance, the teal and pink blend and echo the lavender.

Assembling and Finishing

What details are left? Beaks? I'll cut the beaks from dark multi-colored fabrics and appliqué them later. Legs? I wish I didn't have to deal with them. Some don't show because the swans overlap. The least intrusive approach seems to be a straight ½" strip. I pin up a few beaks and legs to get the effect.

Segue

The quilts in this section form a sort of segue in my work—a transition between the techniques used in my previous quilts, which were pieced within a grid, and later quilts, which were sculpted and appliquéd.

When
background
just use so

56

Hart Celebrating—Energy from Unit Design and Placement

Hart Celebrating
by Joan Colvin, 1993
Bow, Washington
59" x 57"

I used traditional piecing techniques for the stags in this swiftly done "Christmas card." I like the joy and the energy it expresses. By designing a lifelike unit and repeating it irregularly, I got the feeling of being in a natural scene. But, like this happy, vigorous herd, I rushed through the snow and ice, leaving a trail of messy places and a few broken branches!

When You Are a Little Older, Darlings . . .
by Joan Colvin, 1993
Bow, Washington
44" x 51"

This quilt started with my desire to illustrate the phrase "fabric in flight." It never left the nest. I did not stay on theme; that is, my bird may be intending to fly, but the fabric itself is not airy or winglike except in the most literal sense. I started with sketches of an abstract, winglike shape. I suppose I was thinking "aero-dynamic." There are lots of possibilities for twisting and turning this design using transparencies and directional texture. I could no longer see this; I saw baby cormorants.

A black-and-white Florida bird, the anhingua, has big, white wing feathers and babies that look like my design. (In some setups, I'm so predictable.)

I used a grid for the bottom half only. Though I kept a grid line across the wing tops, the wings flow loosely downward. I sculpted and appliquéd, rather at random, the white wing feathers over darker flow-ing feathers.

I had been experimenting with bleach to give plain fabrics tex-ture. One piece, a blue, had turned a peculiar color. During the process, a fold of newspaper or tape left a dark, beaklike shadow. Irresistible to use that as a shadow behind my bird's beak.

Shadow? There must be light—a moon. Impossible, but we let ourselves be fooled. Find the best place for a big moon. A bad bleach splotch can be covered to form a halo around the moon. Nice. I've es-tablished a mood that will permeate the whole scene. I want to encour-age the illusion of being up high in a tree over a moonlit, marshy lake. I try a little harder to find triangles to add to the "lake" as reflections. Darkening the nest area helps.

What if I attached some silk ribbon to add glamor? As I attached the silk, I worried a bit that the ribbon was too glitzy and flimsy and thus not well related to the rather heavy cottons I'd used. What if I lined the ribbon with a dark maroon cotton? This approach provides weight and unity.

This quilt did not soar powerfully into space. It was, in fact, an earthly situation, grounded. This is how I described it for display (I could just as well have been referring to my process): "Here, as the nest-lings watch their glorious mother prepare for the evening, I hope you will experience the tension between the joys of night flight in a lighted sky and that feeling when you are stuck in the nest once again...."

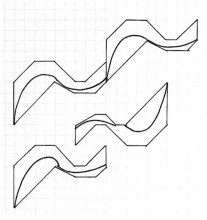

Winglike shape

Diatoms and Wrinkled Whelks—Contours

Diatoms and Wrinkled Whelks
by Joan Colvin, 1994
Bow, Washington
70" x 45"

This piece was a quiet study—not serious, not a struggle—a random cluster of shells mixed with the sand and debris of the beach. I love its border and the sweeping quilting lines.

The striations of these pale, lavender shells suggested strip piecing, which is how I started. But as I stared at the shells, the gently sloped, slightly spiraled edges held me. Do you know the feeling when you want to straighten someone's tie? I wanted to sculpt those shells and push those straight strips around a bit. For me, a ruled straight line is one that I just haven't had time to curve yet.

For background, it seemed natural to use enlarged sand particles, dots, crystalline structures, diatoms—symmetrical fabrics. Laying them in as if painting, sweeping across my fleece, I began to enjoy and appreciate the space of white fleece left bare—the chinks of light that give life to a watercolor.

Imagine the dark backing sticking out around the edges while I was in the quilting process. I got used to it being there. No border I could devise was in any way so satisfying. The piece needed the rough edges in the same way it needed the uneven shell edges. So why not? I used a straight border on the back for firm outer edges, then appliquéd the sand on top, folding it under randomly.

Part II

Designing with Sculpture and Appliqué

This is a freer, more sculptural approach that satisfies my longing for touching, draping, and forming fabric into curving configurations. There are few straight lines and few templates. I simply fasten the fabric where it lies most gracefully. The good news is that this approach satisfies my tactile sense like nothing else. These quilts have a fluidity and a liveliness that are hard to achieve other ways. The bad news is that the moment I begin to actually fasten the fabric in place, it loses some of its life. Speaking practically, it uses much more fabric and is harder to hand quilt. (The stitches tend to get lost in the thicknesses, so machine quilting makes more sense.) Worst of all, the total surface tends to weigh unevenly, as you would expect. But still, I love it.

There are no patterns for the quilts in this part of the book. I've been working on these in between pieced quilts, and over time, I've changed a bit in technique and approach. Different, but not better or worse. The first four quilts are part of a series, "Today Mother Nature Loves . . ." Think about playing outside in the wind or playing inside with paper dolls and looking out—seeing all the things that happen to trees and grass and light as the seasons change. . . .

"The Rose Tree" and "Beach Walk" are my way of celebrating the magnificence of antique fabrics. Keeping the elements simple and focusing on special fabrics made the work seem effortless. I present these two pieces here because I have used this sculpture and appliqué approach as a way to preserve and treasure small pieces of antique fabric.

"~~In Search of James McClane~~ No Longer Looking for James McClane" is about choosing a title and guiding the viewer's perceptions. Finally, I have included an excerpt from my working journal for "The Kelp Queen." You will quickly get the idea for working in this fashion on your own.

I sometimes cross over the line in wishing to share my delight in gorgeous things. I try to reach the optimistic child inside each of us, hoping that overt and sometimes blatant prettiness will help soothe and counteract the disarray around us. I ask myself, "Would I have stared at this before I grew up? Would I want to be here, in this place? Am I drawn into this picture?"

Today Mother Nature Loves Autumn Best

*Today Mother Nature Loves
Autumn Best*
by Joan Colvin, 1993
Bow, Washington
60½" x 72½"

Leaves and wind ...

Today Mother Nature Loves Spring Best

*Today Mother Nature Loves
Spring Best*
by Joan Colvin, 1993
Bow, Washington
77" x 61"

Blossoming trees, cherry
trees, especially old ones ... Think
of old trunks and new pale pink
flowers.

Today Mother Nature Loves Summer Best

*Today Mother Nature Loves
Summer Best*
by Joan Colvin, 1994
Bow, Washington
71½" x 63"

A cool, hidden place in the
woods . . .

Today Mother Nature Loves Winter Best

*Today Mother Nature Loves
Winter Best*
by Joan Colvin, 1994
Bow, Washington
61" x 71"

Pale light, scattered . . . a cold
late afternoon . . . grace and assur-
ance . . .

The Rose Tree
by Joan Colvin, 1993
Bow, Washington
32" x 48"

In "The Rose Tree," I started with a treasured piece of indigo-dyed antique katazome fabric from Kasuri Dyeworks. By folding and draping it into a garment, I could avoid cutting any but the already damaged part. All of my color choices were meant to enhance the subtle, faded tans, ochers, and indigo. I chose other fabrics to symbolize a timeless international figure: contemporary Thai cotton, old raw silk, and fine American and Italian cottons.

Beach Walk
by Joan Colvin, 1993
Bow, Washington
33" x 47"

In "Beach Walk," I found a place for hand-painted silk I took from the lining of a very old kimono. The rough, natural tan cotton for the coat the woman is carrying came from inside an obi.

I formed a sweater of raw silk, a skirt of tissue silk (again from a kimono), and background features with naturals from America, including acid-washed jeans.

Framing this with a silk liner but without glass, after stretching it over foam core, helped smooth out the quilting lines as well as the fabric. I like the effect.

In Search of James McClane

No Longer Looking for James McClane

by Joan Colvin, 1995

Bow, Washington

45" x 52½"

When this face emerged on the muslin, I thought of her as someone searching. I had hoped she might be related to me through the only unknown in our family—a handsome great-grandfather named James McClane. He came from the Isle of Mull, arriving in this country with only a small, locked box. He left a few years later, taking the box with him, along with his other secrets.

But as this person watched me do rocks and waterways around her, I came to find her gaze quite solid and rather self-possessed. Soon I realized she was through waiting for James McClane—and my first title would not do.

Of such mysteries do we create family legends and fairy tales. Ambiguity compels and encourages us to fill in our own details, make up our own answers. A child is intense about it: "Who is she? Why is she there? What will happen to her?" The answer, "I don't know," will not be enough. You'll have to say, "Well, I think she is . . ." and if you use your imagination, the story will engage you both.

The artist controls how much information will be given by choosing a title and writing an artist's statement (which may or may not affect the viewer's relationship to the work). This is the last part of your creative effort; it deserves the same care you gave to what went before. You have an opportunity to *guide* the viewer's perceptions.

In this particular piece, there is considerable ambiguity as to location and era. I chose ingenuous, almost childlike fabrics, yet the effect is quite compelling. I take her seriously. There is patience and tenacity in that quiet look. I am still not sure who she is, but I want to be invited into her world.

The Kelp Queen

A piece of shiny kelp washed up on the beach this morning.

This is not normally an event of importance, but today I thought fleetingly of the kelp queen ... Did she start with my mother, my sister, my cousin? Certainly, I passed her on to my daughters. Where are those pictures of my little girls?

Douglas V. McClane

Here you see a very happy kelp nymph:

But here ... Here is the kelp queen, swelling with the power she senses from the elegant garment around her. In the first picture, she is poised and full of vision—the essence of queenliness. In the second, assured but benign, she is ready to tackle the practical affairs of her court. Notice her arms.

How I'd love to catch this—the essence of feeling queenly. A big part of it, we know, is in the grandeur of the scene—established once again by fabric (in this case, shinier than satin with a life of its own). The magic of how it drapes and folds envelopes and enchants us. Can it be so simple, that something outside of you could affect your inner sense? You are what you believe you are. Is there any clearer proof than in this picture?

I am awed by the power of photography. No way could I duplicate these pictures. I have no intention of using them for anything but to get me in that dreamy state where I can imagine the life of a kelp queen.

What would surround her? What is her relationship with the kelp? Is this idea too bizarre? I'm loving it, though, and I'm thinking of kelp beds I've seen—swirly pictures of stems and bulbs. I don't dislike that brown-green shade, but sunlight through water can do interesting things to color. I'll play with this vision for awhile.

I don't want to set myself up for a big crash. Did you hear me say "catch the essence of feeling queenly?" I'm just going to draw a face and fasten on some fabric. It's not going to be "the essence" of anything. But I'm going to feel like that queen while I'm working for a few weeks, and I'm going to try to make something beautiful enough to keep the kelp kingdom alive and thriving in my head. If it engages me, maybe that will come through.

November 1, morning

Sitting here with my cup of coffee, thinking about the kelp queen. What do I know for sure?

The queen . . . I still love the idea of floating hair. No doubt the concept will run its course, but it's a natural here. Looking through my fabrics, I have a couple of green and gold choices for hair. Fine.

The kelp . . . I glance through a book on brown algae; doesn't sound too appealing. What I think of as kelp varies from the big bulby kind to hundreds of other kinds that have little air sacks or floats. I can use all shapes and colors of undersea plant material and it would all be algae of some kind. So much for authenticity. Let the fabrics intertwine themselves.

Possible fabrics for hair

As well as being spectacularly beautiful, kelp can be tall and thick and ominous. I intend to stay well away from that darker image. The child enrobed in kelp believes in the beauty of this world, and I seem very anxious to preserve for her the image of delicacy with grandeur.

I think the queen will be holding onto strands of kelp.

I want to see the effect of sunlight coming through the blades of kelp near the surface of the water. Try for some transparencies? At the bottom, I think I'll just have some rich gold and green and whatever else works for a floor. That's such a pretty, lacy network where the kelp attaches. (Or it could be; it's sort of gross washed up on the beach.) But it would be a place for darks and other patterned fabrics that contrast with those that are closer to the light.

I do a very quick color sketch.

Stop to consider. Kelp is shiny, transparent. Do I do this literally with satin and silk? I could. But it is tempting to try to get the same effect using cotton. I'm using, I think, cotton for hair and for water. Well, I'll stay very open on this. I might intersperse. There are too many choices here and I'm excited to get into it. I don't know yet.

Back to the kelp queen … What is she wearing? In the water, the kelp blades grow upward, toward the light. So there is no obvious intermingling of the kelp blades with her clothing. The queen can have on whatever I like. Perhaps ribbons of lots of things. Those little floats could be a series of beads. Now I can hardly wait.

Where to start? I'm focusing on her and her garden. I guess I'm not really seeing a kingdom. The kelp queen's kingdom could be huge, with sea nymphs, coral columns, and vast interiors lined with anemones. I'm not really into Baroque though. I'll stay with the single figure, see how big it gets, see how much can happen just with the plant-life concept. I have all sorts of seaweed pictures in my head; that should be enough to fill a lot of space.

Plan of action? I'll do some faces until one is "right for the part." That process can go on, apart from lining up fabrics, which I'll start as soon as I have a quiet morning.

Working sketches

November 3, morning

I scare myself with wanting this piece to be wonderful and being afraid I will misuse the fabric somehow. What seemed clear and sort of a jolly project the other day now seems important to me, and I'm a little tense over it. That's dumb.

I do a couple of loads of laundry, turn the lights on bright, and start thinking. What's the first step, technically?

I don't want to plan and sketch any more than I already have because then I'm telling the fabric, "I have a place for you, and you get cut to this shape to fit it!" That is more the feel of an English formal garden. Not that I don't love that concept—it is just not what I'm doing today.

So, I guess I need to pick some chunks of fabric and lay them out.

Possible fabrics

What if I start with the fabric that I think could suggest the kelp bulbs, then somehow draw the queen's face in relation to it? If I were doing a portrait, I'd have to measure this relationship before I started, then measure the relationship of the head to the whole picture to decide how big the head should be. That I don't have to do all this is the appeal of fantasy figures.

I'll audition fabrics on the floor for now. I expect I'll eliminate a lot of fabric, then I'll pin what I've selected on the design wall when I get going. If I do. I hope.

I've been working on faces. One is a bit too introspective, which is nice way of saying "vacant looking." Another is too glamorous. I just want one I like, sort of ageless and caring. There should be a little concern and worry there, but it should show someone at peace with herself and alert to her strength.

November 4, morning

Sitting here looking at fabric. It's kind of a dark day, and I can't get enough daylight to be sure of my choices. But I have high hopes for this pile.

Fabric possiblities, randomly placed

Fabric possibilities rearranged

I have a moment to think about my plans. Am I doing this for myself or for someone else? In a way, I'm reading to my children again. Some of my happiest days were spent doing that, and I'm thinking what childlike beautiful worlds are possible. But children are honest and direct. They like detail and information as well as magic. Is that the flavor or mood I want? For now, think about the power of a queen or naiad, the physical appearance of the strands and blades of kelp, and how to show the kelp swaying under the surface of the water. Maybe this will be plenty; it seems so. I may get redirected as I work, but for now, I'm going to let the fabric lead me to the composition, letting it suggest how it might work in this scene.

Looking at the design wall, I see colors I like a lot. I've rearranged them while thinking.

Probably half of the fabrics I've selected are hand dyed, bleached, or marbled. Only three or four of the fabrics are "in focus" (high-contrast prints). Now I'll have to stare at all of the fabrics for awhile to see which need to be together. (That is, which fabrics have a natural affinity for one another by virtue of texture and color.) I like to weave one fabric into another in some way.

I give no thought at all to value. I will let the values emerge and develop. Later, I will need to make sense of the scene and pay attention to where lights and darks are needed.

For now, I see several water fabrics that could bring light from the surface: a gold group and a blue-green group.

I have a cluster that will be kelp blades. They are the yellow-green color I need for realism, and they tie in the mustard and green marbled fabrics.

Golds and green-blues for water

75

As to the lovely, dark olive green of my snapshots, see where the sun-light shines through near the legs and bottom ruffle? The color is a warm terra cotta that I think could blend with brown and maroon to give me something quite acceptable. I have two fabrics that make those blends, and with delight, I notice they include chartreuse—these will be important pieces, I think, though they may be put on the sea floor to anchor things down. I see one pattern that reminds me of the kelp holdfasts I'll need down there.

Already, I can see that I've got the darker values at the bottom. The floating kelp bulbs will probably come on top of these fabrics, then I'll work up toward lighter values. I'll stay open to the idea of a ray of sunlight or something that will allow some diagonal division or diversion.

A thought: in-focus prints are usually in the foreground. I had just forgotten for the moment that looking back into the water there could be a haziness (I don't want murky). You can tell I'm not a scuba diver, and it's been a long time since I swam with my eyes open. That will help sort out my water fabrics.

Maroons with golds and greens

November 5, evening

Spend time experimenting—color for kelp, shape, and color of the stalk. How big? What about dimension? A tube? Perhaps too slick and snaky. Don't want that. Ribbons appeal. Yes? No? How many? How wide? But look at the reverse side of several frond fabrics; there is nice contrast. Manipulate the fabric.

I'm too sleepy to do anything other than watch and observe effects as I move things around. I'm working in dull light, which gives an idea of value and color entirely different from daylight. This is not a time to cut anything. But I'm becoming familiar with the fabrics, working up to imagining what the queen is wearing.

I like the idea that the kelp bulb fabric is made to order in some ways, with the bulbs (pears, really) in the right colors and the turquoise back-ground. But the color is too deep for the watery colors I'm using, so I'll have to nudge it lighter with appliqué, applying lighter water on top and cutting out here and there to let water show through.

November 6, evening

I worked and worked today. Woke up early and decided I could do a better face—and I did. I toyed with faces of older women—I'll do that one day—but now I'm looking for a younger woman, one who is poised and wise, though still a sprite. You'd think I was doing a portrait for the White House. The process is almost the same in that it takes intense care and focus. I use freezer paper to help stabilize the fabric for drawing, but the pen can still stretch the fabric surface. This is a tiny piece of wiggly fabric, and one stroke too many can ruin what is, at best, a tenuous product.

I know that I have to like her and that when I do, everything else will begin to flow. I have a queen face now; I won't tell how many I threw away. I know where to place the head on the hair fabric. Now I can actually start to pin fabric onto muslin.

I've been rearranging fabrics; I'm going to eliminate the turquoise. My plan is to use warm maroon, pink, and rust for the floor; pale green for the upper water; and yellow-green to gold for the kelp blades. I have to deal with the brilliant green around the bulbs. I'll watch it out of the corner of my eye.

Some people would eliminate the marbled fabric, looking for clear, pure light. I just can't. I like it, and I'm hoping I can use it to simulate sea grasses or other algae in the distance. Those weird pieces of fabric are what keep me at this, and it's a challenge to use them. I do not always do it successfully, and I am the worst at falling in love with something border-line. But it's my choice.

I've spent all day pinning fabric to muslin and fleece. I washed and ironed a 60" x 90" piece of muslin and pinned it to the fleece on my design wall. I will be sticking pins through the muslin into the fleece. When I'm ready to assemble the quilt, I will repin to catch only the muslin. Temporarily, I like the stability the fleece affords.

Some connections are beginning to work well up close. I assess the composition from thirty feet away:

Color: I try to get used to the colors I've chosen. I am surprised to be working in green and pink. (That's what I see from a distance!)

Value: Pretty much medium throughout; lighter at water surface. Kelp stems will provide dark lines. Queen's dress may need to be dark as well; her face will be the lightest.

This mock-up is really, really rough:

Wendi Colvin

Composition: My little sketch is holding its own. The kelp blades seem to be taking up the top of the composition, and that's okay (imagine tree branches or a vaulted ceiling). There will be plenty to shape and curve.

The key decisions are the placement of her head and torso, the placement of the kelp bulbs, and the placement of the top of the sea floor in relation to the water. Everything else will fall into place.

My muslin is bigger at both top and bottom than I would expect to need, so I know that I have lots of room for the design to flow. However, I think I will place the fabric for her torso on a separate piece of muslin so I can rearrange her clothing and reposition her up to the very end.

I toy with the idea of using shiny French ribbon in her dress. It may be too obvious, but it may also be lots of fun and give me the variety in texture. In the meantime, it is wonderful for helping me determine the flow of lines and fabric. (I may keep some on hand for future sculpted pieces—if I ever do this again.)

I've also taken the time to sort out some fabrics that I may be able to use to show transparency in the kelp blades. I doubt if they will be at all accurate in terms of value and color mix. I like the fun of faking it, using whatever I have on hand.

So there it is, rough as can be, and no one could ever see what I see in it. Today I made great progress (for me, anyway)—I went from disparate hunks to a coherent ordering of color and composition.

This is the first hard step, but it is the most satisfying. I'm euphoric. I look at this mess of lumps and droopy strips and feel great because I see something gorgeous. I know that I'd better enjoy the moment—the hardest part is still ahead. This piece will seem to get progressively worse because the detail work I do from now on will not measure up to the vision and expectations I have at this rough stage. I will keep trying as I always do, and I will enjoy the process, but I've probably reached too far. This is a good-news, bad-news stage.

Working with Transparency

Working with transparency means that if I overlap a piece of clear blue plastic and a piece of clear yellow plastic, the result is probably a pretty, clear green. But it's not that simple when you're trying to overlap olive, rust, and chartreuse. Figuring out the color of the overlap is a challenge, especially since I'm working with opaque fabrics.

For those who are interested in working with transparency, I highly recommend Judi Warren's classes.

November 7, morning

I'm going to take a break from this piece. It's still of powerful interest to me, but I'm tired and I'll need a full head of steam to plunge into the next stage. I will let my energy build up until I'm pulled in irresistibly. Also, my house needs attention, and I have travel plans.

From this point, I begin to work with less vision and more engineering. I haven't lost interest in or enthusiasm for this design, but the remaining decisions are no longer grand and sweeping. For example, "Use yellow-green rising to the surface." Now they are practical. Which piece of yellow-green fabric? Cut where? Is there enough for this part? Exactly how should it be fastened?

A planner/designer works with an engineer to develop a prototype. In quiltmaking, we are both the planner/designer and the engineer. We need to welcome both aspects of ourselves.

"You can't do that, Joan," the engineer says.

"Of course I can; I have to," the planner/designer responds.

With my quilts, the planner/designer wins, often at some cost to the project. When the engineer has a brainstorm, we are both delighted. The engineer good-naturedly views herself as master of the quick fix.

Isn't there another component to this? Aren't we also the technician who, with varying patience and competence, is willing to spend the hours necessary to see these works into completion? I love being that person, too, with the work laid out before me. I'm not too closely supervised, but I've been given general constraints and guidelines: "Quilt water in a wavelike horizontal, following lines in the fabric and joining other lines where they meet naturally." The technician will be around till her eyes cross.

November 18, early morning

I think I'll be able to stay home and work all day. It's clear, cold, and frosty, so in a few hours I'll have sunlight. The scraggly strips on the wall look pretty depressing at this point. I've brushed the dog, ironed some napkins, made some quick stabs at housekeeping, and still the needed action is not happening. I want to work, but I'm pacing.

It's a funny thing; I walked on Oregon beaches last week, and each morning at my feet were huge bunches of kelp, a little different from ours. And the botanical pictures I've been working with were misleading. Kelp stalks are very narrow at the bottom, tapering up toward the top. The hold-fast (at the base of the kelp) is smaller than I'd remembered. The power is at the top, near the bulb. The blades are smaller, almost delicate, where they're attached to the bulb. I guess I've never examined that part closely— usually I get no further than the flamboyant ruffles. Maybe I'll play with this connection.

I'll have a few bulbs put together by the time I have full sun. I can tell that making these connections three-dimensional is going to be too realistic, almost snaky. I'm going to go smaller and try to weave together some strands using appliqué. (A real bulb has eight strands.) My mood is to feel the fabric as I twist it around. At some point, I hope to get beyond the literal.

Later, full sun

I've made some of the blades narrower; they fit in better with the French-ribbon. Now I need to get serious.

Am I going to place the blades on the muslin, then cut and interrelate the marbled water? I have so little of the water fabric that I need to be sure before I cut. There is no point in working on top of the water pieces as I have them pinned on now. Guess I'll take the water fabric off the muslin.

I really need to work on the kelp queen. Her body position may change everything. But the bouquet of stems can change position with her; the ceiling of blades won't change.

The sea floor is tremendously active. The ceiling will be too. I like all the fabric. I've got way too much going, but I love it. I will remove, cover, and smooth as needed later. Maybe less is more, but I can't know now.

I'd better plunge back into arranging kelp directly on the muslin, pinning it wherever. I'll try to consider transparency as I work. That will take the bulk of the sunlight.

Evening

I've spent most of the day at this. I tried to stay with the kelp, trimming it smaller and deciding what overlapping blades would look like positioned on the muslin. I watched it as I ate lunch and had trouble with the brightest

yellow-green, so I added some of the same beige tones I used for the background water and some warmer rusts. I'm happier with a little less brilliant color. We'll see, though. I can always put it back.

I can't go further until the queen is formed. I study arm positions, then make a rough newspaper mock-up so I can estimate her size and the direction and flow of her body.

While playing with ideas for her hair and ornaments, I found four tiny squares of an unusual beige print that have possibilities for a crown. They look like antennae. This seems more compelling than the flowing green hair.

She is pinned up on the design wall. She was a mess most of the afternoon; at various times, she looked like an Egyptian mummy, a tacky night club act, and a statue of Auntie Mame. I think I can pull it off now; I've got a better mood. At the last, I loosely pinned some yellow-gold and maroon fabric and some ribbon onto the torso, and somehow it works just falling, casually. Why get involved in the dress-design process when this simple effect works?

November 19, early morning

Having coffee and staring at this thing. It doesn't look much different from last week, but I know that it is. I've tacked up everything all over again and have a clearer view of what must be done. Today is going to involve less vision and more engineering. I think I will take the whole thing off the wall and lay it on my table because I need to really spread out the kelp blades and get serious about where they lie. After I've pinned them, I can rehang and assess it.

I can tell I'm feeling a little pushed by Thanksgiving, among other things, so I need to stop a second and remember that if I'm going to work well, I need to focus.

What was (or is now) the aim of this design? Capturing the feeling of queenly power was a tantalizing thought, but not one that I as the engineer took too seriously. But capturing some elements of the qualities of kelp and posing some imaginative possibilities as to underwater events were objectives that I could reasonably expect to attain.

Now that I recognize this, I can see two or three entirely different possibilities in fabric and color—something to come back to.

I need to go ahead with what I have here; let the engineer get to work and give the planner/designer a rest. The engineer has a clear set of working instructions. Her solutions must preserve the movement and flow, balancing the literal with the merely suggested.

November 20, early morning

Probably I have an entire day again. Around midday yesterday, I put the composition back on the wall to continue placing and pinning background, gradually defining lights and darks as I worked. I notice that I'm using my little sketch frequently to check out major movement. The colored spaces are different, but the sweeping movement, from top left downward through the body, is still there.

I'm ready to take the composition off the wall and baste the areas I'm relatively sure of. This forces me to make decisions about places I'm less interested in. That's how I keep momentum sometimes.

Two things:

- I can refine the queen later. I know exactly where she will be placed, so I will take her off and make that a separate project—sometime when it's peaceful but when I have less than a whole day.
- The pieces pinned on loosely give off nice shadows. Am I using those dark lines to visually "give bite" to the composition? They won't be there soon. On the other hand, the whole thing looks very busy and active; I have assumed that finishing will settle it down. Here's when you can't know till you see; and you don't want to see till you know . . .

Well, I am going to plunge in and baste today.

I have limited myself more than usual by using the fat quarters of marbled fabric for background. I had to cut them up to extend them, and so they are where they are. (I can re-emphasize them by adding kelp blades.)

If I can get it all basted, I will start to appliqué. Machine work may be possible to anchor edges. There are no leaf lines in kelp—worse luck. It's like looking through Jell-O!

I need to do everything I can today to have this stage over. Refinements will continue throughout, but the heaps of fabric all over and the general confusion are getting to me.

November 20, midafternoon

The upper two-thirds is now roughly basted; some inner background seams are whipped together (perhaps permanently). The fleece has gradually fallen away, leaving the muslin alone to hold everything.

I stopped basting at the point where the floral bottom begins because I need to press it, lay it out, and see what kind of side measurements are likely, then position my uncut floral fabric to square it up. I can slice off the muslin where the one large piece of floral begins because this floral will be sturdy enough to take appliqué, and I want it to permeate the entire bottom third of the composition. It has become a keynote fabric.

I need a totally fresh start on refining the design. I will wait till another day. I expect to rearrange several background lines, fill in chinks with no fabric, reposition the queen, and get serious about the sea floor (now totally haphazard with possible patches of fabric pinned loosely). Hope I still like it next time I look.

November 21, morning

Said I wasn't going to work, but how could I resist a sunny morning? I rearrange kelp slightly and straighten out the bottom.

The sweeping movement can be emphasized with light. Light from the upper right needs to sweep down across the figure and curl upward on the other side. The hazy contemporary fabric I've chosen for water in the upper right has patches of light that direct the eyes down as far as the figure. From then on, I can use refining details to continue the flow of light—maybe anemones and highlights on the gown.

Viewing the composition from a distance, I'm afraid this is going to be hideously ugly if I don't do it right. I'm going back to black, white, and tan for my next quilt! This is wearing me out. I have too many medium values. I need more contrast so her arms don't jump out. I need to let it go and get some honest opinions, mine included.

November 27, evening

I'm at a new stage. I was not happy with this at all and was beginning to think I had gone off in the wrong direction with color. Looking at it for these few days helped immensely. My sister said, "I've never seen one at this stage when it is so rough and active/busy. It's confusing, but the colors are going to be rich and lovely."

She said she'd like to see the blue-green of my sketch (for which I'd substituted striped emerald weeds). I tried a section of smooth shades of tan to teal, and I had to agree that it gave the calming touch needed. I will use fewer weeds and less emerald.

I add some darks for punch and some lighter rusts at the ends of the blades, leaving the center areas yellow-gold. I'm gradually covering up the chartreuse.

I took the afternoon to begin finish work on the queen. I will try to work in an outward radius, everything in relation to her face. My dithering will have to stop. It's time to put this thing together.

November 29, morning

A book appeared in the kitchen. (I am sometimes in that room.) Last weekend, someone must have been reading my dog-eared copy of Zen in the Art of Archery. I had marked pages 50, 51, and 52.

> You do not wait for fulfillment, but brace yourself for failure. You think that what you do not do yourself does not happen. Learn to wait properly, leaving yourself and everything yours behind you so decisively that nothing more is left of you but a purposeless tension....
>
> Eugen Herrigel

Right. My deadlines are self-imposed. Breathe.

November 30, afternoon

I spend a short, sweet hour or so refining fabric in the upper third of the composition. It begins to look rather peaceful. In the process, I remove the dark ribbon I'd added to the blades. That is still optional; I'll decide later.

I drape some of the ribbon stems to check out bulb placement in relation to the body. It will work. That will be the very last step, so I'm going to remove all ribbon except that on the dress.

The sea floor: I think anemones may be better than elaborate sea-floor life. Where I can, I use the patterns on the fabrics to simulate the anemone stalks and intersperse these with tentacles. I add a few anemone stalks to satisfy my desire for absolute clarity.

The hard work is done. In snatched moments over the next weeks, I'll assemble it; then there will be another assessing period (before layering and quilting) where major changes could still happen. After Christmas . . .

Why am I so drawn to the literal? Throughout history, the art world has been slightly disapproving of the romantic literal. Calendar art and illustrations were cheap art. But I adore it. The Pre-Raphaelites, Arthur Rackham, the mystical approach, fantasy . . . it is the same desire to "see" that draws others of us into science fiction.

I am perfectly capable of trusting an object to be there in the abstract, and that, too, is satisfying. But when I am working, I want to see the outside and the inside and everything about it that I can imagine, and I want to celebrate the best parts.

I am not going to be the bearer of bad news. That's probably denial in today's terms, but I don't think so. I didn't say bad news doesn't exist. It just doesn't hold my attention during the time when I have a choice.

December, here and there

The engineer made a technical decision. Since I was using ribbon with an overcast edge, it wouldn't be inappropriate to use machine overcast on the rest as well. And it would be so much faster. So, I fasten down all the cotton fabric, using Roxi Eppler's machine-appliqué technique. (See "Book List" on page 116.) She presses all her edges carefully first. Most of mine were basted in place.

I redrape the ribbons for stems and finally choose where to stitch them. I long to have the weedy fabric back again—it gave a better sense of depth. My friends thought that one area could be confusing as to whether I had

water or sky there. My compromise was to extend the floor, fading the growing sea leaves (ostrich plume hydroids, really) by using the reverse side of
the fabric and slightly coloring it with pencil, and adding just a few weeds.

I refined the dress, crown, and placement of the outer edges. A bit of
trapunto discourages wrinkles in the face and arms. For continuity, I use
trapunto with the kelp bulbs too.

You gain a little; you lose a little. To avoid making the design look
ominous, I got a little too delicate. My friends who've experienced the deep
kelp forests of Northern California will not relate to this "bouquet."

I find myself loving the sea floor, which came easiest and with almost
no thought at all. And with the merest nudging, the castlelike background
emerged unexpectedly from the rather amorphous drapery fabric.

There were some technical difficulties that I will try to avoid in the
future; for example, I divided the face from the neck instead of staying with
one piece of fabric. I may be pushing it here, but I don't feel like doing it over.

I have no idea how to border this. I'm sure a dark value is too heavy; a
medium gray may do it. I'll experiment.

Later

The border is in place! It was not easy, and I'm beginning to worry
that borders seem so difficult for me. Sometimes I can just skirt the issue by
not having a border if the design stands by itself. But this quilt needs some
sort of frame, I think, like an old portrait.

I tried all the dark, light, and medium fabrics. The medium fabrics
seemed best. I had a subtle tan stripe that was working all right. I kept
wishing for a golden tan like the background fabric but without a print. Yesterday, I bought a piece of cheap, green-gold cotton. I sprayed it with diluted
bleach to soften and enliven it. Whoa! Underneath was a tannish pink.
Happy surprise. A medium value, it seemed to go innocuously with everything and sort of echo the general color scheme.

I was about to go for a simple dark binding when my neighbor dropped
in. She agreed with the new border choice and casually said, "What's that
stripe over there?"

"That's just my pile of old obi's . . . Oh, Mary Lee, you've got it. That
stripe is perfect for the outer edge."

At least we think so. The richness of the old silk bolsters the home-made border. The total effect is a little different, yet stays quiet and satisfying. I'm done.

Six months later, July

In making "The Kelp Queen," I tried too hard. I put her away for several months. The day I unfolded and looked at her coolly, I wondered if she'd appeal to me. Yes and no; I still love my idea, but I could have done it better.

After all that work, I picked up my fabric markers and made changes to her face. I was prepared to start over on the face but didn't need to. I improved the arm position slightly after staring at mine in the mirror. Why couldn't I see that before? I was personally involved and not fearless.

August 18

As I prepare this quilt for final photography, I am still pulling and fussing over her head and neck. They're too stiff; I don't feel relaxed with her. I need to determine why right now. This is my last chance.

First, the head is too puffy. All right, I can undo it, pull out some stuffing, smooth, and reappliqué. Second, the head feels too stiff on the shoulders, although anatomically, it checks out. The crown is good, but I miss the softness of hair in front. Pull out a piece of bright gold and green fabric; drape it a little. I CAN'T BELIEVE THIS. I LOVE IT.

I spread the fabric around her face. When I stand back ten feet and assess, the fabric provides a firelike splash of color that balances her white skin, and even better, it hints at being transparent over her shoulder. The watery green ties into the composition. A few more beads entwined and, oh, do I feel better.

Just "OK" does not seem to be enough for me. Once again, I am saved by some instinct. LISTEN TO YOURSELVES, MY FRIENDS, YOU KNOW THE ANSWERS IF YOU CAN JUST LISTEN TO THE QUESTIONS.

I am left with the desire to make her again someday, closer up, finding an adult relationship with the concept. This one was childlike, to speak to a child, and I treasure it on that basis. Was a lot of that dithering wasted time? Maybe. But the experience hurtled me, propelled me toward the last series in this book, where I worked swiftly and cleanly over a three-month period in a wholly different approach.

As I reread this journal and see how unsure I sound, I am struck by how the best parts of my work are effortless, hardly mentioned.

The Kelp Queen
by Joan Colvin, 1994
Bow, Washington
57" x 76"

Part III

Designing Fast and Fluid

I am aware of a stronger need for fluidity and naturalness. It emerged in my early quilt-design efforts as I pushed and squeezed past little blocks. Until now, stylization has been an appropriate and, for me, immediate entry to the joy of design. It's just that sometimes I am made restless by this, as if I were afraid to face the issue. I am looking at something so grand, so intrinsically beautiful, that I must approach it head-on. To do less is to trivialize the subject.

It is a risky thing, though, to face something you know must come out very right or be very wrong. You don't win; you just try to get close, try to catch a swift moment or two when you think you glimpse something of the vision you loved. These moments may come when the fabric hangs loosely and splendidly, and you mentally fill in some lines and spaces. Sometimes I see briefly what performance art is about; you can't expect to pin down this joyful moment—it's enough to have had it.

This last group of quilts began with a desire to move swiftly from concept to conclusion. That is, I wanted to marshal and focus energy, gain momentum, and complete an idea within a short span of time (say, a week [night and day]—excluding the gathering of fabric, final appliqué, final quilting, and border).

I'm testing the idea that I can gain fluidity in my work this way, by working in broad sweeps. I want to see large movement, large contrasts, and unity from good design (not necessarily from the repetition I've used and liked). This, for me, is a return to painting with a broad fabric brush. Any technique that accomplishes my goal is fair game.

To remove diverting temptations and to intensify my gaze, I have chosen two restricting devices. First, the subject matter must be something I know by heart, such as heron or trees. (I counted 189 heron last week on the beach.) Second, I will be led initially by a keynote fabric, which I will study until it speaks to me.

Sometimes in quiltmaking, we go off on learning tangents for years. It's no different from real life. Sometimes it takes a long time to learn something simple. You do not have to improve with each composition. Don't fall into the trap where you think someone is assessing your development. They're probably not. How will you know you are at a dead end unless you try it? How will you stay on track? It can't be determined what sort of track you've left until you are dead and gone. If you are bothered by this, I recommend reading Art and Fear by David Bayles and Ted Orland, and Bird by Bird by Anne Lamott. (See "Book List" on page 116.) You'll feel a lot better.

Trumpeters at Dusk

Trumpeters at Dusk
by Joan Colvin, 1995
Bow, Washington
24" x 24"
(Collection of Ruth
Chappell)

I reduced and simplified the tundra swan unit pattern for this small quilt. Gold-threaded mauve obi silk became the evening sky, and various mauves blended with it. The aim was to do a rich, simple blending of fabric in a very small space to evoke the opulence of old oil paintings.

Sometimes the trick is to be led by the fabric; leap at what the patterns and textures have to offer.

Choose Your Values
by Joan Colvin, 1994
Bow, Washington
53½" x 71½"

I had been immersed in
grand landscapes in New Zealand,
Alaska, Canada, and Yosemite
and had come home with a beautiful piece of hand-dyed fabric
from Alaska Dyeworks.

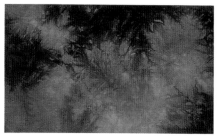

Staring at its colors and twists, I thought of mountains and re-flected lakes. I spent three precious days folding, draping, and other-wise trying out skies and lake scenes. In the end, there was no punch, no center, no focus to my compositions. Scenes can be ordinary, and mine were. Stop when this happens. You have to learn that.

Later, when I saw the little trees sideways as branches, it seemed so obvious. Laying strips of treelike textures between strips of sky, I began to get a sense of the lighting. There was so little!

It was very early morning, and the barest rays of light made a showy spot. I was developing a very narrow value range. Any speck of fleece showed through like a car headlight.

So, the available light established the mood. I felt I must walk without snapping any twigs.

When I realized that trees don't have to match up or be ruler straight, my assembly concept seemed as simple and clear as the design. At some point, it occurred to me how to square up my vertical edges. I had one flexible tree of kimono silk that I could sculpt into a barklike texture. Perfect. I scrunched up this tree fabric until it was a nice width and the vertical edges were parallel.

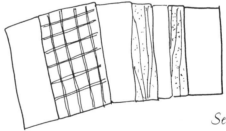

Seam random strips.

I'm looking at the photograph of my mock-up on the design wall. I'm seeing it as a whole, as a composition in and of itself. Now look at the finished quilt. Which do you like better? The mock-up has the look of a kimono and the sense and feel of the ornamen-tation that we so admire in that era. The upper line across the top has life and movement. Do you see why some fiber artists eschew the preciseness of a traditionally finished quilt, with all the i's dotted and t's crossed? The trick is to know what is needed when we are working.

Draw up until vertical.

Heron

Woodblock

Heron Woodblock
by Joan Colvin, 1995
Bow, Washington
47" x 58½"

Here is a wonderful, unexpected quilt that resulted from a gift of large-scale black-and-white fabric, beautifully printed. I had a small strip showing black and creamy white feathers and leaves. The print flows freely, but it is drawn quite precisely, and the feeling is formal—definitely not feathers for heron as I know them. But then, could I extend the fabric by sketching my own black lines on muslin? Where would this lead? Could I then design a heron, exaggerating to include these fanciful printed feathers?

The idea led to a sense of the old etching or block-printing process, essentially black and white, where the ink sometimes doesn't quite cover the paper. The concept allows me to preserve the fabric's sense of formality and dignity but also to soften and diffuse the busyness and intensity by spreading the fabric out over a larger surface and injecting a range of neutral colors.

Working with Special Fabric

When you have a small piece of special fabric and you can't afford cutting errors, photocopy it (make lots of copies) and use the paper until you make a final decision.

Virtual

Madrona

Hazel Ayre Hynds

Virtual Madrona
by Joan Colvin, 1995
Bow, Washington
47" x 72"
(Collection of R. Gene and Esther Grant)

I love red ocher. Here I'm looking at a square of it, dyed by a neighbor, Judy Robertson. It veers off into chartreuse on one edge. It's not too great a leap to see the rich red trunk of a madrona.

Take photos of madrona trees—peeled, smooth, the flavor of them. Showcase the subtle dye changes by allowing large unbroken stretches of fabric—those trees are messy in places, but your eyes are drawn to where they are exposed and nakedly satin.

When the uncut Nancy Crow fabric began to resemble an incoming wave not yet ready to break, I added sand and stayed simple for the background. Where to stop? I'm never sure.

The result, to me, is incipient power, clean and hard-edged.

Hazel Ayre Hynds

Alders

Alders
by Joan Colvin, 1995
Bow, Washington
42" x 70"

I used to think of alders as those trees that densely cover everything and remain thick, shapeless juveniles long past reason. But I've
begun to see them grow old and tall, rising above the ordinary.

A composition of straight trees is quite common; there are thousands of ways to do it and thousands of people have. No matter; I can't
get these trees out of my mind. I will go for the simplest-possible concept: a large weaving in which the horizontal marshland and vertical
trees intermesh here and there.

I have too many fabrics that might qualify for trees. I could
choose a number of lighting schemes, each with its own mood. But I
find two hand-dyed fabrics that work with an alder-leaf print batik, so
I decide on inky blue with dark rose and tan. (The gray blue and pink
need the warmth provided by golds and tans.)

The fabric I choose has to do the job with color, texture, and
value. And I want a wide assortment for breadth and variety. Because
there are so many out there, and because we can make our own if need
be, a fabric that is somewhat symbolic or evocative of the scene or subject has an edge.

I decide to use the fabric semi-literally. My leaf-print batik can
simulate actual leaves by virtue of placement. But I won't cut the
leaves out or place them on branches. This would seem contrived and
stiff. I want the quilt to stay ambiguous.

I opt for swirly drama in the trunks, which are almost too lush in
texture when viewed up close.

I like it that I sometimes see this quilt as a firestorm. But the light
in the early morning and late afternoon can produce fiery effects in
more benign settings. I can feel the undergrowth and uncertain footing
as if I were tramping through these marshes. This is a simple composition, but not a serene one.

Red-Tailed Hawk

Red-Tailed Hawk
by Joan Colvin, 1995
Bow, Washington
43" x 49"
(Collection of Max
and Sharon King)

Here is a splotchy gray-and-white, hand-dyed piece that is asking to be pen-embellished. I'll try. It's relaxing and I'm seeing feathers. They aren't long enough for heron feathers, but there are other local birds.

When I remembered the red ocher left from "Virtual Madrona" and saw the identical striations in the tail of a red-tailed hawk, I was committed to try.

I have trouble suggesting or making a large, real creature abstract. I thought I would use random strip piecing for the wings, but as details got more realistic, I began to think that I'd build him up feather by feather. In the end, I wanted to pick up this bird, fluff him up and down, and put him back on the branch more buoyantly. How can a creature be composed of tiny, stiff, almost straight parts and still airily rise and expand? I'm learning.

Silk Lake
by Joan Colvin, 1995
Bow, Washington
48" x 59½"

I chopped and extended a cheap camouflage fabric to resemble foliage. Two harmonizing fabrics for the water were interesting enough to stand alone in large amounts. The total effect is serene and simple, rather like a serigraph or screen print. The antique silk water is enhanced by a silk damask frame.

Silk

Heron

Silk Heron
by Joan Colvin, 1995
Bow, Washington
42" x 52"

This morning I am looking out at grayish Puget Sound. I still love the imagery evoked by earthy hand-dyed fabrics. And I'm still trying to combine my own drawings with fabrics that enhance them (or the other way around). I have two colors of silk dye that I like—gold and gray—the others are all too bright for now. I also have some silk from the inside of an antique kimono. I'd love to see what brush strokes could do. This is an experiment; I've not done brush painting for years.

Pressing the silk lightly onto freezer paper, I do several heron and finish them off with pen detailing. Some I leave with very little detail. What looks pleasantly delicate up close becomes ho-hum from a few feet away. Boldness is required. It's a long way from a few satisfactory strokes to a finished composition.

But dive in. Place one silk heron body on the design wall and choose fabrics of all sorts that enhance, not overpower, the delicate gray green. Bits of magenta have bled out from the ink in a tiny edge. I can try to use that color subtly.

This fine transparent silk (which I'll never find again) is just wonderful. It will mold into and onto other fabrics, leaving a gentle edge. My desire right now for a liquid feeling is satisfied by the enormously forgiving properties of this material. It softens, blends, shields, and shadows.

I am getting the misty, foggy feeling of the morning shore—rocks and tide pools are forming, and the silk seems to welcome anything I propose. The basic idea is happening in the way I'd hoped.

Adjusting, emphasizing, omitting, and highlighting all come later with no more or less confusion than usual. I learn here and there—things for next time. Relaxed realism. Implied accuracy. Don't analyze the perspective, the proportions, or the reflections (so hard for me). Let the fabrics play against each other and fall as loosely as possible while relishing the *idea* of what really happens in nature.

The moments of focused, effective energy are fewer than I'd like. As I gain design experience, I also learn to recognize my peak creative times. I may actually have more time than I used to, but I want more.

I'm becoming better at assessing the composition during the working process. I'm also becoming more courageous in my designs and more willing to rip out and redo. That's new.

I've recently learned to recognize when I'm restless or dissatisfied with a design element. Not too long ago, I might work vigorously to patch up a bad place, and sometimes I could. But more often, lately, I can say, "This part is wonderful, but that part is second-rate. I dislike that part." Then I wait . . . A better idea usually comes.

Here was my fabric. A sweeping, speckled piece that, among other strange strokes, had a fine set of heron legs. Play with that. Find a body in proportion. Build the surroundings to take advantage of the speckled, now sandy area around the legs.

I'm off and running.

I love this quilt, probably because the colors are rich and well integrated, and because I still get a certain amusement from finding ready-made fabrics that work in unexpected ways.

Heron in Reeds
by Joan Colvin, 1995
Bow, Washington
50" x 54½"
(Collection of
Cindy Tims
and Steve Skelton)

Part IV

Evaluating Your Work

Most of us have concerns—maybe worry—about juried events or peer evaluation. We wonder whether or not we really have the experience/expertise to assess and evaluate our own work. Who among us doesn't ask, "Do I really know what I'm doing?"

The Assessment Process

What happened? How did you miss a problem? Were you hurried? Did you really look at the composition, or did you see only what you expected to see? Were you unwilling to make needed changes? Sometimes, you know something isn't perfect but hope it will work out. More often, the problem hadn't appeared when you assessed the quilt. Later changes affected that place without your noticing. And sometimes, you just can't give up that part. You let yourself fall in love with it.

I think that we each need to learn to assess our own work with detachment, that is, a neutral gaze. There is a level of working that you reach when you are "really into it." When you are involved at this level, you are aware, alert, watchful, and critical, yet at the same time, nonjudgmental. You are watching your work unfold—measuring, comparing, and looking for snags. It's difficult to reach this level with people looking over your shoulder; they may be drawing you back into a judgmental state, where you worry about what they think of you and your work. All of us, though, have friends in whose company truly useful and astute observations are made, and work progresses. (This is because they, too, are into the matter at hand—not watching you work, but watching the work take shape.)

You are lucky if you have already dealt with what I've described. This concept has been around for centuries. It just makes sense as we go through it ourselves. As long as we understand what is happening, we can have moments of, if not maturity, at least serenity.

Using the Elements and Principles of Design

What are the working tools for assessing designs? I can tell you mine. I ask questions about unity, movement, contrast, spatial relationships, negative space, and color at various viewing distances. (See "Appendix A: Elements and Principles of Design" on page 117.) These are the elements that have stuck with me over the years and seem to be handy tools. Other people have different lists. It is well worth your time to explore design theory. Internalize what you can, then make your own working list. (Like tennis lessons, you need to learn the basics. But if you stop to look at your wrist position while you're playing, you become self-conscious and things don't go right. My point is that you must internalize these elements so that they're there when you need them, while you are working.) It takes a little time for these elements to become an intuitive part of your process, but at some point they will.

To help you understand what I mean, let's take one of the elements and explore it a bit. I use the phrase "spatial relationships" as shorthand for the concept in which I try to understand the relationship of lines to the shapes they make. How tall is the heron? How wide? How much taller than wide? How long is the beak? It looks too short to me. What is it standing next to? Is that object a believable size? Have you checked to see if the distance from head to belly is right? What about the distance from belly to feet? Look at the object itself. Recheck yourself.

That is what is going on in your mind as you try to re-create an object or image. But you don't need the words. If you are drawing or sketching an object in front of you, you are measuring without words. You are guiding your pencil with little intuitive assessments. "Does this line go all the way up? No, move it over; it meets that line about halfway." Stop drawing. Now ask yourself, "Does it look like a heron?" Yes, but a fat version.

There are two assessing processes here: the process of drawing and measuring and the process of naming and identifying. You may recognize Betty Edwards' theory. Her book, *Drawing on the Right Side of the*

Brain, was a bombshell in art education. She proved what any artist knows: phones, people, and other miscellaneous interruptions stop the art process. She told us why artists stop themselves from doing good work. She also told us that anyone can learn to draw with sensitivity.

What are the implications for you as a quiltmaker? Learning to draw is good for your mind, even if you don't really need drawing to sew. It is not beyond you if you are open to it. If you can measure, you can re-create any shape.

Most fine art is the product of imperfect, personal, exaggerated measurements that come from the combined impulses of that unique person. Visions are not often in proportion. If you aren't intent on re-creating a recognizable object, the pressure is off, and you just have to like or not like the relationships between lines and spaces. You don't expect to see them in any special, identifiable way.

Betty Edwards put a very cogent twist on this process of re-creating an object. She was concerned that in drawing a leaf, for instance, you would expect to see a certain kind of leaf and fail to really look at the one before you. She wants you to concentrate on the shape and the details of the leaf in front of you so that you are focusing on where the lines lead rather than thinking "leaf." She is concerned that the identifying and labeling part of your brain will flash leaf and leaf symbols (all the ones you've seen before) and distract you. She wants you to be preoccupied with the edges, flutes, and veins of only that leaf. That is what we call "really seeing."

Line Study, Driftwood
by Joan Colvin, 1994
Bow, Washington
22" x 28½"

But in quilt design, symbols (the idea of a leaf) work well. We are often looking for instant communication rather than re-creation of an actuality. We know that Bow Tie, Pineapple, and Tulip block designs are exactly that—readily identifiable symbols.

I would like you to think about designing a simple shape after a long look at the original object in all its complexity. You need to fully understand what it is you are simplifying. To encourage you a bit: primitive art does not come from people with simple perceptions. It is the emotional outpouring of someone who has looked long and hard at nature's intricacy. That person is simply unfettered by some of the conventions we pick up. The power and sensitivity are there.

Taking Advantage of the Mathematical and Artistic Sides of Your Brain

Here is one very practical lesson from Betty Edwards. Developing a pieced design based on an arrangement of squares and triangles engages the mathematical or left side of your brain. Thinking about color, movement, and texture engages the artistic or right side of your brain. I tell my students to build their object on the design wall quickly, using any fabrics. Then, stand back and begin to refine the components.

Assessing at Various Viewing Distances

Viewing distance, which I refer to as an "in and out process," is discussed in every design book and almost every quilt book. You must have a way to see your work at various distances. Use a peephole, a camera viewfinder, photographs, binoculars held backward, or squinting. This is the most basic assessing process known.

You need to like your work at very close range. Is the design (your block, your unit, your center of interest) intrinsically pleasing? Is the interrelationship of your design units—the position of the repeats, the interlocking of units, the larger designs they set up—good? Colored, textured fabric is there for a reason. Was the reason a good one? Does your assembly technique detract from the design? (It's often necessary to redo, reappliqué, restitch, and otherwise neaten up areas that just barely survived the struggle.)

Assess the relationship of quilted lines. Do they help hide seam lines you wish could disappear? Do they extend naturally from the design, or do they impose a restricted pattern that isn't logical?

You need to like the whole composition from mid- to distant range. What lights or darks do you see? Is the total mass of each pleasing, compelling, or disturbing? Would you be drawn to it from across the room? What colors are predominant? Have several merged into something unexpected, something that should be highlighted or perhaps mitigated? Do secondary and tertiary patterns weave through, and should they be emphasized or de-emphasized?

As you look at your work, are you stopped, bothered, or interrupted by something that doesn't seem right? Try assessing the composition from various distances. From mid-distance, you'll see negative space and other snags you can't see up close. You may pose a question here for which you have no answer. Let it work in your mind for awhile. If you need advice, get it.

> *Confusion and clutter are failures of design,*
> *not information.*
> Edward R. Tufte, *Envisioning Information*

Avoiding Common Problems

By thinking ahead, you can avoid some specific problems.

ঌ *The finished spatial relationships and/or visual flow are not as good as they were before assembly.* Did you remember that seam allowances can change proportions and ruin the plan for large-scale pieces of fabric? Though you think you've allowed for this, you may have subconsciously become accustomed to, for instance, a spot of yellow on a seam allowance. Artists from other media can be fooled by this when they work in fiber.

§ *The finished work feels too tight or constricted, but it looked fine on the design wall.* Loose, unquilted fabric often moves, reflects, and shines nicely. Loose pieces cast slight shadows that, in your mind, become part of the composition. Allow for this; you actually may want dark fabric in these places. Remember that freely flowing portions can be done on a separate base so they can be repositioned or rearranged. Do you need some curving lines? Can something be woven throughout by using appliqué or by enhancing a secondary pattern?

This problem can also be related to what is lost when seam allowances disappear: the whole composition tightens up. Maybe you need an extra row here and there. Never skip the step where you work with the finished-size unit on paper or computer. Rethink your borders.

§ *The texture or color fades away or looks "blah."* How does a fabric read from a few feet away? Can you still see the texture? Are your changes or combinations too subtle? Do you need a broader range of color to enliven or enrich? You might refer to books on color to help identify problems, or look at your favorite paintings and photographs for fresh ideas.

§ *An entire section looks blah.* Generally, this problem happens in an area of the quilt that hasn't particularly interested you. If you identify such a place, make one decision first. Is this a neutral area meant to be calm, to offset more active vibrant areas? If so, perhaps it is too big. Perhaps it is not interconnected well enough, that is, doesn't lead your eyes into the design. Perhaps the neutral idea isn't a good one—more is needed. It may be uninteresting because you lacked information and detail (in color, design, and texture) that propelled you to do interesting things. Your vision was too vague.

If it's not too late, rethink that part and inject some fresh ideas. For instance, look at photographs to see how colors interrelate. Tear out portions of magazines with ideas that could blend in or complement what you already have. Look at the neutral areas in photos, noticing values, textures, and colors. You just need fresh input.

❧ *Strange patterns emerge.* A lovely relationship between fabrics has unexpectedly connected with something else. Sometimes textures or values merge into weird configurations. You aren't always aware of this possibility when working. You are more likely to see issues related to color, rather than value or texture, as you work on the design. Correct with overlays if other changes can't be made.

❧ *Triangles, squares, and blocks are awkwardly placed.* Happens to us all, all the time. Check values and color. Change an awkward shape by adding or subtracting components. Use triangles to point or to aid in transition. Try breaking up squares with a triangle here and there. Rethink the spacing between objects. Appliqué corrections if need be.

❧ *The finished work feels top or bottom heavy.* Squint. Which area feels too heavy? To get an instant feel for the composition, draw rough diagrams of the light and/or dark areas. Try adding length or width to these diagrams. (This may convince you to add to the quilt.) Redo areas in different colors or values. Appliqué little somethings on top. Add units. It's never too late. And perhaps most basic of all, rethink your outer borders. Try cropping as a photographer would. Add to or chop off. I rarely do borders or make final decisions about my outer edges until I have a chance to look at the design as all the components come together.

❧ *You lose interest in the design.* Think about this for a moment. Why does it happen? First, it's best to drop a project rather than force it when you have no heart for it. If you have no regrets, there is no problem. Some regrets? Well, let's see what you can identify.

> • **Could it be that the design is intrinsically poor?** After living with it a bit, it couldn't sustain your interest. Drop it.
>
> • **Is it too complicated for your abilities?** Could it be pared down, simplified?
>
> • **You weren't sure what you originally had in mind.** The idea fizzled. Next time, spend more time

Keep your interest vital and moving. Recognize that fixing something later is a risky plan—because we have infinite, incredible patience while we are working, but when we have emotionally pulled back, we have almost none.

on the vision and let more excitement build up before you start. Jot down your vision and your hopes for it. Think about different ways to implement it. Have more ideas than you need before you start. Try working smaller. A simpler concept is more physically manageable. Set a deadline. Try to stay focused, working swiftly and connectedly.

- **You switched to something more interesting.** Can you view the dropped project as a stepping-stone to the new one? If so, it really did serve its purpose.

- **The thing fell apart somewhere along the way, even though you thought you were working with vigor and your ideas were excellent.** Now you hate the finished quilt and feel discouraged and betrayed. This is familiar to us all. Talk to a friend about each element that you thought would work. Did it at all? Partially? What can be saved? What could be changed? Try drastic cropping. Is it possible that you'd prefer to take what you've learned to a fresh version of the same theme, converting that frustrated energy into something positive? Such an experience can propel you forward to study and research, and sometimes to produce your best work.

- **The finishing details you'd imagined don't measure up.** You are all done and these last little decisions are taking way longer than you'd planned—you're frantic. You've heard me say, "That's a finishing detail I can decide later." But I've proved to myself that somewhere along the line I should stop to experiment—make sure that I can design an effective beak and so on. Don't cling to a plan that should be discarded. Sometimes an idea born of this sort of frustration will be far better than the original! Be willing to say, "This is really bad. What else could I do?"

- **You like your concept, you think it is going well, you want to work, but you are using every excuse not to.** (I iron napkins I won't need till the following year and get very interested in sorting out runs in my pantyhose, making labeled packages, etc.) For whatever reasons, you need fresh energy and inspiration. There is nothing wrong. You are still working well. Perhaps you are experiencing a bit of boredom if you've come down from a design high, when you were vitally and totally absorbed. Now you can only see hard work ahead. Try entering the working process by solving a very tiny problem. This can alleviate anxiety and get you back into interesting larger problems.

- **Is it something indefinable?** How many times have you turned to the help section in a manual only to find that everything is covered except your problem? In this case, there really isn't a guide. But if you have read this far, your staying power and sense of humor are sufficient to lead you to decisions on your own. *Don't be afraid to wobble through problem solving.* Isn't that how it's really done? No part of the physical process is too taxing or beyond anyone. It's the staying power that counts. It's something inside that has to know, has to see. In this state of mind, it is difficult to rest until the answer is at hand.

One Last Thought

A perfect quilt is rare. As you get more discerning, it becomes rarer.

Enjoy a quiltmaker's body of work, and enjoy the atmosphere and the fun of presentation. Whether it's show-and-tell at a guild or a fiber-arts display at a museum, take each quiltmaker seriously, respecting that person's level of expertise. Treat yourself the same way, and remember the process you loved or struggled with as you worked.

What we do in our quiltmaking is a private exploration that will indeed lead us along convoluted paths. Following a tantalizingly personal vision, putting multicolored concoctions together until you can taste them, and adhering only to the rules you like are probably not part of the framework within which your mother sent you out into the world. And a steady diet of such rich mixtures would no doubt leave you exhausted. But, my friends, when the mood is irresistible, and you decide you are hungry, you do know where the cupboard is, don't you?

If you aim to dispense with method, learn method.
If you aim at facility, work hard.
If you aim for simplicity, master complexity.

Wang Kai, "The Mustard Seed Garden,"
as recounted in *The Way of Chinese Painting*
by Mai-Mai Sze

Resources

Sources for hand-dyed, -painted, and -marbled fabrics:

/106

Alaska Dyeworks
300 W. Swanson #101
Wasilla, AK 99654
(907) 373-6562

FLAIR
Marlis Kuusela
487A Highway 9
Sedro-Wolley, WA 98284
(360) 856-4988

Just Imagination
Judy Robertson
PO Box 83
Bow, WA 98232
(360) 766-6885

Book List

Bayles, David, and Ted Orland. *Art and Fear*. Santa Barbara, Calif.: Capra Press, 1993.

Colvin, Joan. *Quilts from Nature*. Bothell, Wash.: That Patchwork Place, 1993.

Dietrich, Mimi and Roxi Eppler. *The Easy Art of Appliqué*. Bothell, Wash.: That Patchwork Place, 1994.

Edwards, Betty. *Drawing on the Artist Within*. New York: Simon & Schuster, Inc., 1986.

_____. *Drawing on the Right Side of the Brain*. Los Angeles, Calif.: Perigee, 1989.

Herrigel, Eugen. *Zen in the Art of Archery*. New York: Random House, Inc., 1971.

Lamott, Anne. *Bird by Bird*. New York: Anchor Books Doubleday, 1994.

Miyawaki, Ayako. *The Art of Japanese Appliqué*. Washington, D. C.: The Asahi Shimbun and The National Museum of Women in the Arts, 1991.

Rybicki, Verena. "Attribution: The Sincerest Form of Flattery." *Quilting International* (January 1994).

Sze, Mai-Mai. *The Way of Chinese Painting*. New York: Vintage Books, 1959.

Tufte, Edward R. *Envisioning Information*. Cheshire, Conn.: Graphics Press, 1990.

Appendix A: Elements and Principles of Design

As I move from my vision toward a finished quilt, I consider certain elements and principles of design to help me assess my work. A basic understanding of them and how they are interrelated will help you as you explore the design process. For any given project, some of these will be critical, and some will have almost no significance at all. Sometimes I deliberately choose to ignore one or more. There are all sorts of considerations in the formation of good design; what follows is a discussion of those I have found useful when designing quilts. I strongly recommend that you develop your own working list.

Unity

Think of the entire quilt at once so you don't get preoccupied with a little pattern that doesn't belong anywhere. You want the design to work as a whole. Repeating a color or pattern is an easy way to do that. Or, try gradating the values from light to dark or using a directional design that points or chases itself. Traditional pieced patterns are already expressions of unity; scenic designs or those that focus on a single object are more susceptible to clutter.

Visual Movement

Where does the eye go? What do you see first? Usually, the eye is guided from light to light; it can jump spaces successfully. For variety, light can be broken up, but if the placement of light areas is too choppy, you will lose the desired effect. The viewer's eyes will tire from whirling around a quilt top with no place to rest.

Be careful not to let the design elements lead your eye right out of the picture. Avoid design shapes that point and lead you to the outer edge before you have time to appreciate the heart of the work. Watch for these as you design, and it will become an intuitive process.

Contrast

As long as we are considering the placement and movement of light within a design, think of how important stage lighting is for spotlighting, highlighting, setting a mood, or giving direction. The placement of light helps create contrast. Rembrandt produced powerful results with just a touch of light on a mostly dark ground. Assess your design idea in terms of contrast: Would a high contrast between light and dark be best, or does your idea call for a smooth flow with little or no break, little or no emphasis beyond the gentle transition of colors?

Spatial Relationships

When everything in a design is the same size, boredom is a possibility. But you can look at this another way: blandness can be very calming. Variation in size breaks things up, for good or bad.

It is important to assess the effect of variety in size in your work. Try drawing a simple diagram. This can help you see what will happen in the whole quilt top. Does the relationship of lines and spaces convey your idea?

You might need variety in size to show off fabric to its best advantage or to leave room for a particular quilting design.

Negative Space

Looking for negative space can be an eye-opening concept, especially if it has never been pointed out to you.

From frustrating experience, I can warn you to experiment ahead of time with how your blocks come together so that no unpleasantly shaped or colored negative spaces develop. In fact, with careful planning, exciting secondary patterns often emerge at the four corners where blocks touch each other. Avoiding difficulty at these places forces me to examine and improve them—a design opportunity not to be missed.

Viewing Distance

Most artists would like viewers to enjoy their work from any vantage point, so it is important that you shift your focus as you work. It is very easy to get absorbed in the design and color-selection process at a working distance (arm's length) and miss what happens when you stand back from your work. For example, the brushstrokes on the backdrop for a stage set look entirely different when viewed from the rear of the theater.

Make sure you view your quilt top from a distance throughout the working process. Shapes and values are perceived differently, depending on where you are standing. Squinting used to be one's best bet. Now you can buy a reducing glass or use instant photography. Zooming in and out is critical to assessing good design.

As you assemble blocks and then join them, seam allowances disappear and size relationships change a little. Sometimes a design looks a little crowded or awkward where large-scale patterns come together. Luckily, more often, it works the other way, and you are delighted by the happy accidents—unplanned side effects!

Room to Play

I like to leave some aspect of my plan unsettled, allowing room to see what happens. This can be a subtlety in block placement, but more likely it is an area where color variation can occur as the mood strikes, or it is a background area as yet unformed in my mind. Learn to balance the risk of wasted time versus the joy of spontaneity. If I know everything about the quilt top before I start cutting and stitching, I am always less excited and motivated to finish it. On the other hand, if I didn't plan carefully enough and it isn't going well, it is hard to stay interested.

What works best for me is to plan fairly well; plunge in and get started; go back and refine; plunge in again with more knowledge and enough momentum to almost finish; assess the results and correct a bit; then finish the top and quilt at my leisure. I also find that if I save some intriguing little detail for the very end, after quilting, I'll finish, and more than that, my creative interest stays alive until the end.

Designing for Ease of Assembly

The assembly process is a personal matter. Some of the most gorgeous quilts are technical wonders, and some are not. I can love and appreciate the exuberance and adventure of a collagelike expression in which nothing matches or touches and all the strings hang out. But I can be deeply moved by the perfection of the work of Jan Myers-Newbury, for example, as well as by the work of immediate friends whose needles are miracles of accuracy and for whom each stitch is a challenge. Their standards for technique are enormously high.

How you will assemble a design is a major decision, involving how you feel about technique, your personal vision of the end product, and your own patience and commitment. (That does not mean you always have to do the same thing!) Read enough about quiltmaking techniques to find a comfortable approach. What follows is the process that works best for me.

I choose easy-to-assemble shapes. I like little triangles and squares because you can use them like large brushstrokes to create movement, and it is easy to sew them together. I like diagonals because they line up, whether large or small. If I'm improvising, I don't care what the angle is, but if I'm lining things up, a 45° angle will take me anywhere I want to go with the design. Diagonals are dynamic lines that lead the eye through a composition.

I usually use one of two distinctly different assembly processes. The first is like making the muslin for an original dress pattern—working loosely, pinning, tacking, basting, changing, and molding. In other words, nothing is secure.

The other process is more like what you do when you've bought a dress pattern—cutting, stitching, pressing, and trimming in the prescribed sequence. I swing back and forth between these two, depending on how much I know about where I'm heading. I've already confessed to employing any expedient solution that occurs to me. I neaten things up at the end the best I can without redoing anything major, and I quilt over lumpy seam intersections shamelessly. Then I move on. That's it. I've had my fun.

Quilting to Add Dimension

Anyone new to quiltmaking may need a little extra perspective here. Some people are less interested in the piecing process than in the quilting to follow. They prefer a single unadorned expanse of fabric and decorate it with stitching lines, making intricate line patterns with some slight dimension. The result of expending years of labor and pounds of thread can be a simply exquisite, textured line drawing on a plain canvas. These beautiful, whole-cloth quilts are highly prized.

Planning the quilting for a pieced quilt, however, requires additional thought. You must consider the design lines in the pattern of the fabric as well as the lines that develop as the individual units are cut out and sewn together. The delicate quilting stitches add a third line dimension. The interplay of these three elements is critical to the success of your work.

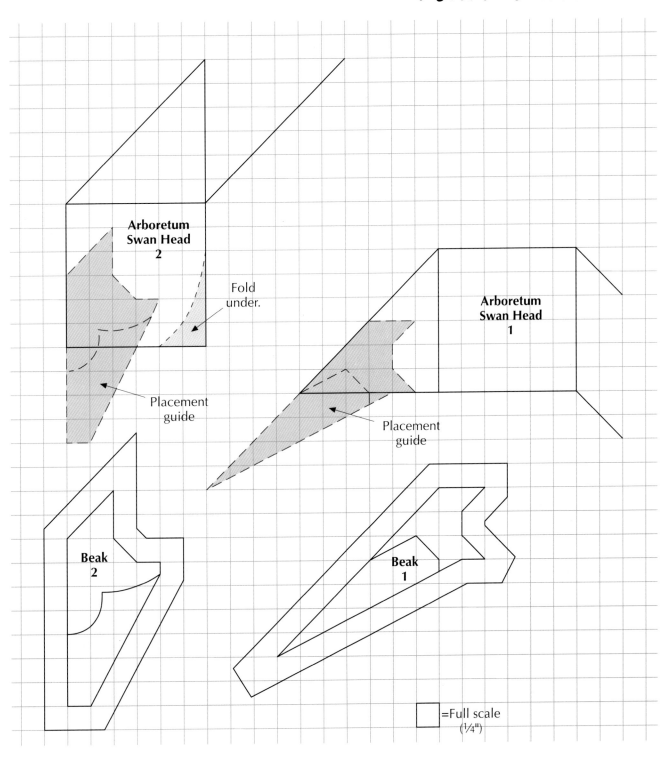

Arboretum
Swan Head
2

Fold
under.

Arboretum
Swan Head
1

Placement
guide

Placement
guide

Beak
2

Beak
1

=Full scale
(¼")

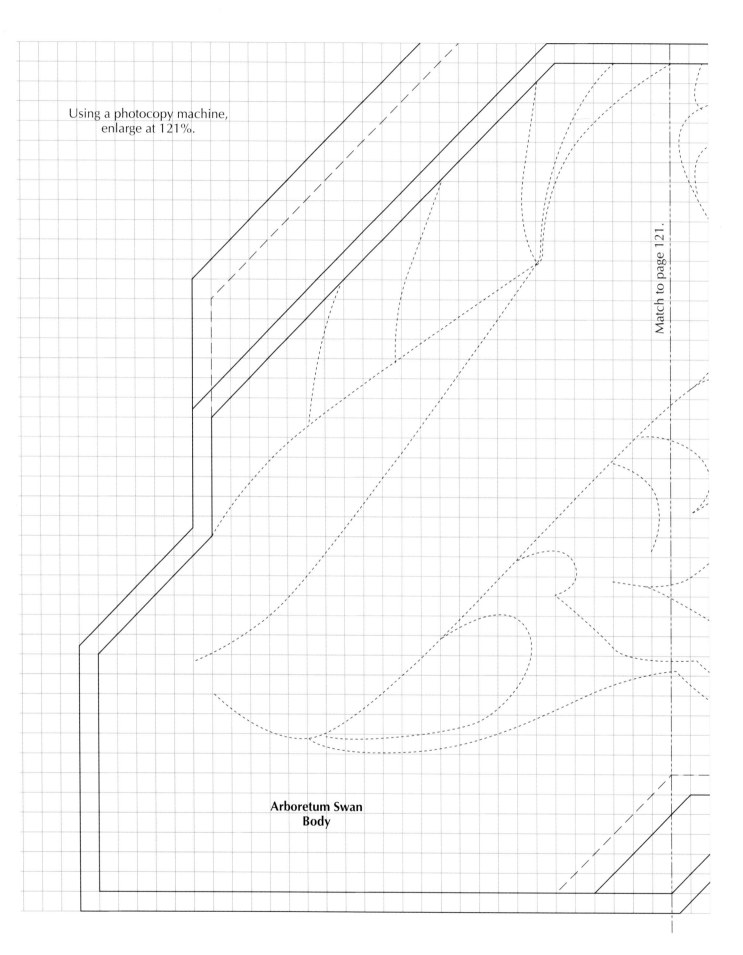

Using a photocopy machine,
enlarge at 121%.

Match to page 121.

**Arboretum Swan
Body**

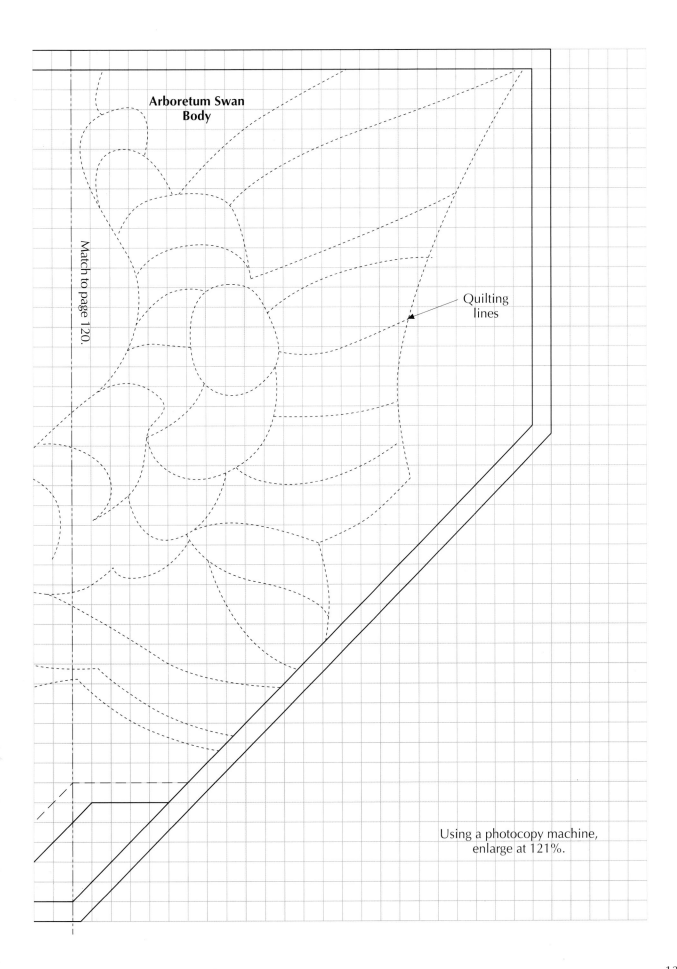

**Arboretum Swan
Body**

Match to page 120.

Quilting
lines

Using a photocopy machine,
enlarge at 121%.

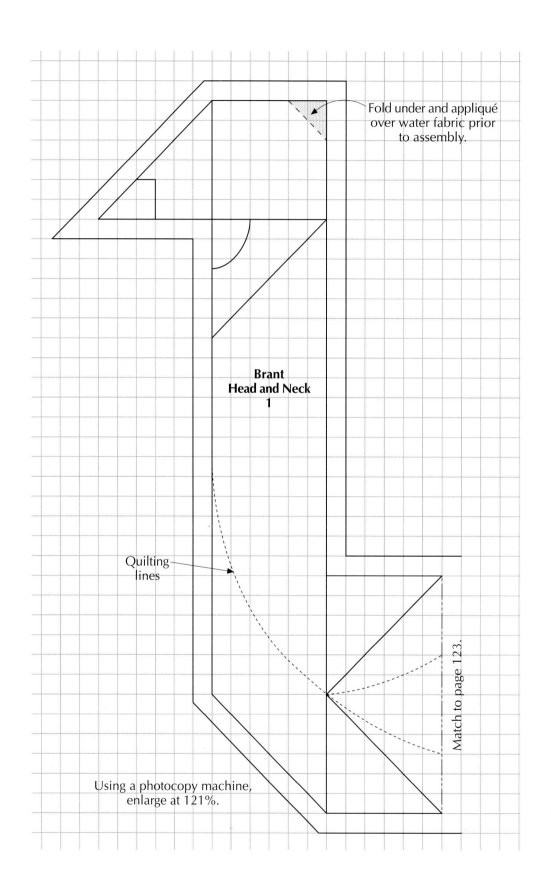

Fold under and appliqué over water fabric prior to assembly.

Brant
Head and Neck
1

Quilting lines

Match to page 123.

Using a photocopy machine, enlarge at 121%.

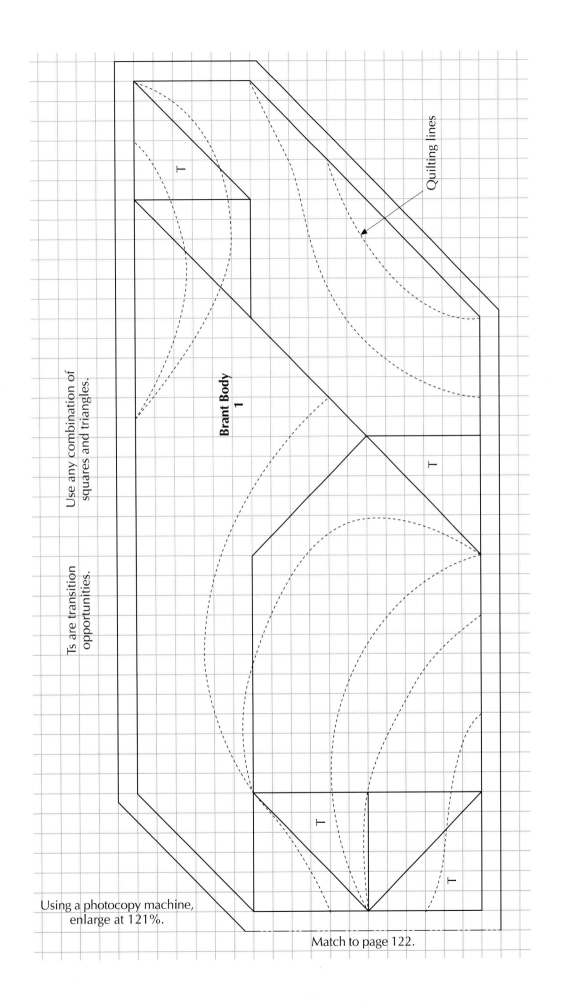

Quilting lines

Use any combination of squares and triangles.

Ts are transition opportunities.

Brant Body 1

T

T

T

T

T

Using a photocopy machine, enlarge at 121%.

Match to page 122.

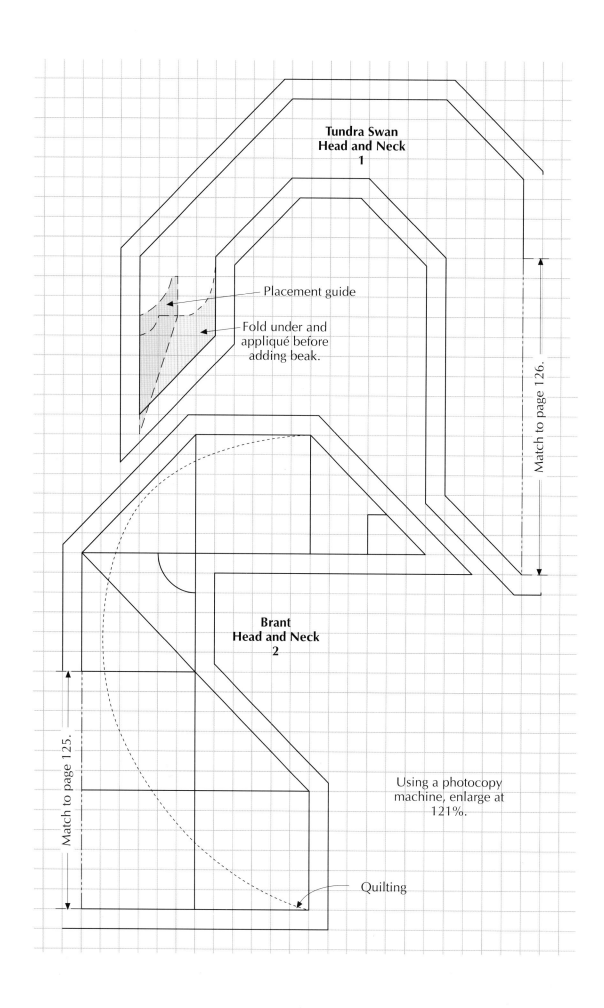

**Tundra Swan
Head and Neck
1**

Placement guide

Fold under and
appliqué before
adding beak.

Match to page 126.

**Brant
Head and Neck
2**

Match to page 125.

Using a photocopy
machine, enlarge at
121%.

Quilting

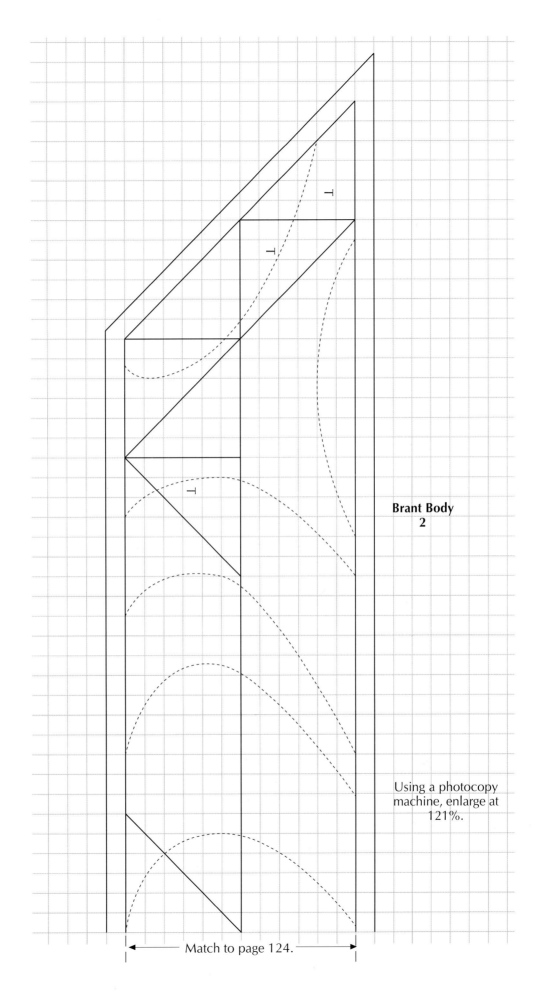

Brant Body
2

Using a photocopy
machine, enlarge at
121%.

Match to page 124.

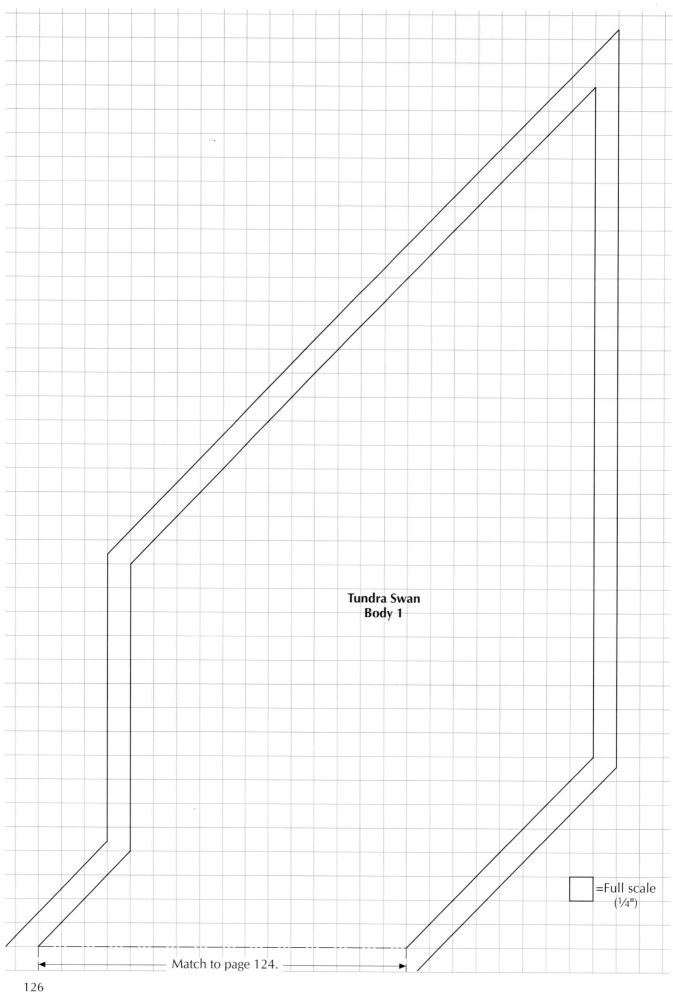

**Tundra Swan
Body 1**

=Full scale
(¼")

Match to page 124.

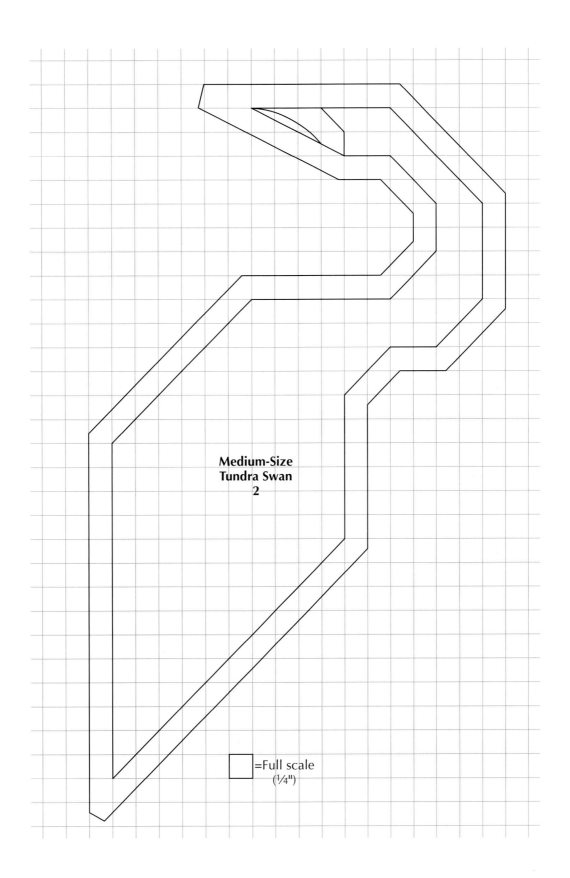

**Medium-Size
Tundra Swan
2**

=Full scale
(¹⁄₄")

Related Titles from
Fiber Studio Press and That Patchwork Place

**FIBER
STUDIO**
PRESS

Erika Carter: Personal Imagery in Art Quilts · Erika Carter

The Nature of Design · Joan Colvin

Velda Newman: A Painter's Approach to Quilt Design
Velda Newman with Christine Barnes

Appliqué in Bloom · Gabrielle Swain
Bargello Quilts · Marge Edie
Blockbender Quilts · Margaret J. Miller
Botanical Wreaths · Laura M. Reinstatler
Colourwash Quilts · Deirdre Amsden
Designing Quilts · Suzanne Hammond
Freedom in Design · Mia Rozmyn
Quilted Sea Tapestries · Ginny Eckley
Quilts from Nature · Joan Colvin
Watercolor Impressions · Pat Magaret & Donna Slusser
Watercolor Quilts · Pat Magaret & Donna Slusser

Many titles are available at your local quilt shop or
where fine books are sold. For more information,
send $2 for a color catalog to That Patchwork Place, Inc.,
PO Box 118, Bothell, WA 98041-0118 USA.

U. S. and Canada, call **1-800-426-3126** for the name and
location of the quilt shop nearest you.
Int'l: **1-206-483-3313** Fax: **1-206-486-7596**
E-mail: info@patchwork.com
Web: http://patchwork.com